BE STILL, MY SOUL

SAM LAING

BE STILL, MY SOUL

A Practical Guide to a Deeper Relationship with God

DISCIPLESHIP
PUBLICATIONS
INTERNATIONAL

Be Still, My Soul

Printed in the United States of America

Cover design: Chris Costello
Interior design: Chad Crossland
Author photo: M. Gregory Murray

ISBN 1-57782-056-8

TO MY WIFE, GERI,
whose life and love draw me ever closer to God.

Contents

Acknowledgments

I, once again, want to thank all of the wonderful disciples who serve so unselfishly at DPI for enabling me, and so many others, to write books that can be of use in God's kingdom. Most of us might never have been published were it not for the encouragement and spiritual and professional counsel of Tom and Sheila Jones and their outstanding staff. The entire kingdom of God owes all of them a debt that can never be repaid.

I also thank my amazingly competent, incredibly hard-working and spiritually sacrificial executive assistant, Tracy MacLachlan, for her help in putting together this book and for her assistance in so many other areas of the ministry that enabled me to take the time to write it.

Lastly, I thank my wife for encouraging me to take a week away from the ministry and our family and go away, out in the country, to author this book. Without her encouragement, indeed her insistence, I would not have done it and would have missed out on the great experience of being away with the Lord, working on this project.

Introduction

He has made everything beautiful in its time. He has also
set eternity in the hearts of men; yet they cannot fathom
what God has done from beginning to end.

ECCLESIASTES 3:11

From the beginning of time, God has sought a relationship with us. He longs to know us and to be known
by us. The story of the Bible is that of God taking the
initiative, of him seeking us out. When Adam sins and
hides from God in the Garden of Eden, God comes looking for him: "But the LORD God called to the man, 'Where
are you?'" (Genesis 3:9). And the last book of Scripture
closes on the same note as the first, with God, in the
person of Jesus, appealing to us,

"Here I am! I stand at the door and knock. If anyone hears
my voice and opens the door, I will come in and eat with
him, and he with me" (Revelation 3:20).

Not only does God long to know us, he has also
created within us the desire to know him in return. There
is something deep inside us all that hungers for the eternal. It is an indefinable impulse, a driving thirst, a gnaw-
ing emptiness that longs to be filled. We may seek to fill
it with busy-ness, with accomplishment, with pleasure
or with people; but none of these suffice. We strive, we

hope, we dream, we aspire. This is largely what defines
and separates us from the rest of creation—it means
that of all God has made in the visible world, we alone
are made in his image. This explains our burning desire
to build, to learn and to extend our lives beyond the
short time that we have on earth.

A very large part of the world attempts to deny this
need altogether, or to fill it with lesser things than God
himself. To do this is to condemn oneself to a life of
emptiness, shallowness and frustration. The quiet misery
of the lives of people all over the world who live this way
bears eloquent and overwhelming testimony to the folly
of striving to live a meaningful life apart from God.

But there is another problem we must face: It is the
problem of the committed disciple who has failed to
come to know God in an intimate, personal way.

I am deeply concerned and grieved by the lack of
spiritual depth and reality in the lives of many in God's
kingdom. There are many who have sincerely dedicated
themselves to Jesus, but who are missing the point of it
all—that all of our work, our zeal and our attempts to
obey must flow out of a relationship with God himself.

What happens to us when we miss the point? We
become superficial. We become actors, merely trying to
do the right thing, instead of children of God, seeking
to *please* the heavenly Father we love. We feel like fakes

and phonies. In point of fact we are just that, because we are motivated by *duty* instead of *relationship*. We can then begin to wonder if everyone else in the church is a fake, too.

When we reach this point, we are but a step away from spiritual collapse; we are headed for burnout. The cross of discipleship is too heavy to carry if we do not do so out of a desire to love and please God. "Commitment to commitment" will not take us all the way to the end—commitment to Jesus will, because that commitment is to a *person* and not to discipleship as merely a principle or a concept.

Without closeness to God, we will have a sense of powerlessness and anxiety. We will feel as though we are on a roller coaster ride: up one day, down the next, since there is no interior stability from intimate, daily contact with God. We will seek to please the disciples around us and will ultimately resent them for imposing upon us a cross that was meant to be borne for Jesus' sake—not theirs. We will seek to live our lives relying on their faith, their strength. This will cause us to have an unhealthy dependence upon other Christians, going far beyond the help and encouragement intended in righteous, godly discipling relationships.

This is not God's way. His plan is for his children to live in a daily walk of personal fellowship with him that grows ever more intimate and inspiring with the passing of time. Thus, Paul could say,

> And we, who with unveiled faces all reflect the Lord's glory, are being transformed into his likeness with ever-increasing glory, which comes from the Lord, who is the Spirit (2 Corinthians 3:18).

This is how older Christians in our fellowship can grow stronger and more zealous as the years pass by, not burning out, but having their youth "renewed like the eagle's" (Psalm 103:5).

∞

I do not remember exactly the day in my young life that I felt in my heart the first pangs of my hunger for God. Perhaps they came to me as a boy who lost his earthly father or as a college student in a tumultuous time in history who saw through the emptiness of it all. I only know this: I had decided early on to seek God and his Son, not just because I needed them for what they could do for me, but for their *inherent worth*. I decided that come what may, I would be close to God. I did not know all that that would mean, and still do not, but I believed that this was the only way to be sincere and real in my desire to be a follower of Jesus. I decided that I just could not fake being a Christian, but that I would have to live this life from the inside out because of a genuine fellowship with God.

During the writing of this book I celebrated the twenty-ninth anniversary of that decision. I look back with profound gratitude to the God who has allowed me to know him, to have intimate fellowship and friendship with him, and who has continued to reveal himself more deeply to me with every passing year. I hope to be able to share with you, in this little volume, some of what I have learned in those years, that you may be encouraged to better know your Father in heaven and in that relationship to be comforted, inspired and transformed.

Sam Laing
Chapel Hill, North Carolina
February 1998

PART ONE

Time with God

Chapter 1

EARLY MORNING TIME

Jesus was an early riser. In a short but telling sentence in the first chapter of his gospel, Mark ushers us into the inner sanctum of Jesus' life:

> Very early in the morning, while it was still dark, Jesus got up, left the house and went off to a solitary place, where he prayed (Mark 1:35).

Jesus devoted the first part of his day to communion with his Father. When you think about it, this was the only way he could have carried on. The pressures of ministering to needy people, the challenge to shape and mold his disciples, the exhausting ministry of healing, the draining requirements of preaching and teaching and the unrelenting scrutiny of critics were his constant companions. How could he have done it, were it not for his closeness to God, a closeness that he jealously guarded throughout his life? As we see his amazing poise, his blazing courage, his tender compassion and his unfailing patience with friend and foe alike, we wonder where he found such reserves of strength—and found them so consistently. The answer is plain: Jesus always stayed near to God, and he devoted the first part of the day to renewing and enjoying that relationship.

What makes us think we can be any different? If Jesus, who was the Son of God and had known God's fellowship in heaven, needed to begin his day with the Father, how much more should we!

We all know the excuses: "I'm not a morning person." "I have to leave for work so early." "I have to get the kids off to school." "I don't want to be legalistic." "I pray throughout the day." But they are just that—excuses.

There is no Bible command I am aware of that lays out morning devotions as an absolute requirement. I can only appeal to the example of Jesus and that of other Bible characters like David (see Psalm 5:3, 57:8 and 59:16) and to the overwhelming voice of logic. I can also share my observation from many years of life in God's kingdom: Those men and women I know who are the most spiritual and who continue to grow are those who are devoted to morning prayer and study of the Word.

How does spending the early morning with God help build a closer relationship with him?

- In spending our waking hours with God, we show the priority of this relationship over all else in life.
- Since our waking thoughts determine the tone and course of our day, morning time with God sets our minds and hearts on what is most important right from the start.
- Early in the morning is one of the quietest times of the day, affording us the chance to concentrate and think without interruption.
- We are rested from our night's sleep and our minds and emotions have had time to recover from the strains of the previous day.
- We are able to clear our consciences of the guilt of sin before we begin our day.
- We are able to cast our burdens upon the Lord before the day begins.
- We are able to draw upon God's power to strengthen us for what lies ahead (Psalm 5:1-3).

Some of us have a hard time getting out of bed in the mornings. As a veteran of this battle, let me offer some practical help:

Go to bed at a decent hour. Undisciplined late retirement is not a sign of being a hard worker, but of lack of self-control. Much of our nocturnal activities consist of puttering about the house, watching late-night television or simply dawdling around. Some of us need to get rid of our vampiric, "night person" attitude and learn to retire at an earlier time, so we can get up before the sun comes up and the day is already rolling along at full tilt. Some of us have unique work schedules, but even so, the first hour of arising needs to be God's hour.

Set a definite time to awake, preferably the same time every day. If the body is trained to retire and arise at consistent times, we sleep better and feel better.

Be responsible for getting yourself out of bed. Don't rely upon your spouse, a parent or a roommate. They may forget. It is not their job. This is the first decision (or the first battle!) of your day—take full responsibility for it yourself.

Do whatever it takes to wake up. If you need scriptural conviction, read Proverbs 6:6-11 and 26:14. On the practical side, I recommend "The Laing Two-Alarm-Clock Method." This is an ingenious (!) plan I developed when I was a sluggard of a college student. It works this way: I tune a radio alarm in to a pleasant station, set it for the time I need to get up and place it on my night stand. Across the room, I set another alarm clock to go off five minutes later. This one is battery-powered (so as to not be thwarted by an electrical outage) and has a piercing, unpleasant alarm. It is far enough away from my bed that I must get up in order to turn it off (and the sound is so disagreeable that I can't bear to let it just run out.) This method has served me well in establishing one of the most important disciplines in my life: getting out of bed immediately and on time every day. The difference this habit has made in my relationship with God is immeasurable.

I also suggest an early morning shower, walk or cup of coffee if you are a bit bleary-eyed when you arise. I preset our coffeemaker to have the coffee ready when I come downstairs, and it helps me to get out of slow motion and into a good frame of mind.

What if we miss our early morning time? If the reason was unavoidable (even Jesus had this happen to him—see Mark 1:35-37), then don't let it ruin your day or your attitude. God is still in heaven, and you will still go there in spite of missing a quiet time! If you missed or were rushed because of a lack of discipline, make things right with God before you head out the door or as soon as you can. Again, don't allow a missed morning devotional time to so frustrate and distress you that you end up sinning in worse ways later. I have known some disciples who were so easily put into a state of bondage and accusation by this that it became a real source of discouragement for them. Get help and advice from other Christians if you need it, and do not allow this to be an ongoing problem.

∞

There is something thrilling and exciting about getting up early. Most of the world is still sleeping. The house is usually quiet. Even the outdoors is especially quiet just before sunrise. We have a quiet sense of confidence in our hearts that we are giving God the place in our lives that he deserves because we are giving him first place in our schedules. The results are so powerful that, having experienced them, I believe you will never again want to neglect your time of morning devotions or relegate them to a later time in your day.

I urge you, for the sake of your relationship with God, to spend time with him daily, "early in the morning."

Chapter 2

QUIET TIME

Jesus deeply valued his time alone with God. We have already seen how he devoted the early morning hour to prayer. Let us expand this thought as we discuss the need for daily quiet time.

Jesus sought out quiet time. He felt the need for isolation and for solitude, and he made sure that he got it. It was his practice to withdraw. His counsel to his weary disciples was to "Come with me by yourselves to a quiet place and get some rest" (Mark 6:31b). It was said of Jesus that he "often withdrew to lonely places and prayed" (Luke 5:16).

There is a need for secret, sacred time with God that is devoted to him alone. Here, no one else is admitted. Here, we can relax, unwind, breathe freely, think clearly and commune without interruption. Occasionally having quiet times with others has its place in helping them or us to develop discipline, or to teach or learn how to best spend the time, but joint or group devotions must never replace our private time with God.

Jesus found the quiet place. He would go out into the wilderness or find a quiet garden in the city (John 18:1-2). He urged that we find privacy within our homes:

"But when you pray, go into your room, close the door and pray to your Father, who is unseen. Then your Father, who sees what is done in secret, will reward you" (Matthew 6:6).

Many of us are limited in our walk with God because we fail here. We do not secure a quiet place. We try to read and pray in a busy area of our home, within earshot of the telephone or television, or where we overhear the conversation of our families or roommates. We are interrupted by those who bustle about, entering and leaving as they carry on their business. Never in this environment can we settle down and devote our full thoughts to communing with God. Let me say it plainly: *If you do not have a quiet place where you can be alone and free from interruption, then your relationship with God will be shallow and limited.*

There are many places to go and many ways to find a quiet time and place. The room with the closed door recommended by Jesus could be your own bedroom, an empty bedroom, a basement, an attic, a study or a sunroom. Perhaps a room with a vista (see Daniel 6:10) can be your special place. Playing recorded spiritual or classical music can transform a plain room into an inspiring spiritual refuge. You may discover that your backyard, patio, porch or open-air deck meets your needs. It may be that a walking trail, a public park, lakeside, seashore, hilltop or mountainside view will become your quiet place. Or, if you are like me, you will find that you enjoy many quiet places and that variety is essential to enhance closeness to God at different times.

Jesus urged alertness. In his final night with his apostles in the garden of Gethsemane, he pleaded with them to be awake and alert in prayer that they might overcome temptation (Mark 14:37-42). Peter, who was there that evening and who slept instead of praying, learned his lesson well. In words redolent of those of Jesus on that fateful night, he admonishes us in his first letter to be "self-controlled and alert" (1 Peter 5:8) and to be "clear minded and self-controlled" so that we can pray (1 Peter 4:7).

Some of us may have a quiet place and quiet hour, but must confess to a shameful lack of alertness. We drift through our quiet time without engaging our full mental, spiritual and emotional powers. This must be called what it is—sinful laziness. Do whatever is necessary to wake up and be at your best for your time with God.

How much time is sufficient? Many disciples struggle with this, and there is on the one hand the extreme of bondage to a legalistic conscience and on the other the peril of weak, shallow laziness. The best answer I can give is simply to impress upon you the investment of sufficient time to build intimacy with God. There should be enough time spent to leave the quiet time with a sense of peace and closeness to God, with a feeling of having been fed by the Word and of having cast the burdens from our hearts. At the risk of appearing legalistic, I would say that one-half hour would be a good starting point, and that additional time should be added (and hungered for!) as we mature in our walk with God. We should also realize that there are seasons of our lives when more time will be needed and other times when our allotted time is entirely sufficient. Leaders who shoulder more responsibility for the church and for the lives of others should arrange to have even greater amounts of time on a regular basis for prayer (Acts 6:3-4).

How should the time be allotted? How do we divide the time between prayer and study of the Word? Here again, the goal of closeness to God should take precedence over legalistic quotas. I try to divide the time equally between study and prayer, but I find that prayer is the absolute essential. Prayer is the most intimate form of communion we have, and it most attunes us with the heart of God. The mistake some of us make is to study for so long that we leave too little time to pray. Thus, we end up more burdened after our devotions than when we began. The solution is simple: Save enough time to pray, no matter what!

Should we pray or read first? Here again, we should make no rule. Our relationship with God should not be allowed to become stale, and we should do whatever is needed to keep it vibrant and alive. Some days (and perhaps for a long stretch of days) I will read first, then pray. But if I sense the onset of boredom, ritualism or a mechanistic attitude, I change the order. I would urge you to do whatever is necessary to have a refreshing time with God and to frequently vary your practices to keep it that way.

The lack of growth in Christlikeness in the lives of many of us bears undeniable testimony to our lack of devotion to quiet time. Our anxious minds, burdened hearts, guilty consciences, uneasy demeanors, our continual failures to overcome sin or conquer character weaknesses and our lack of evangelistic fruitfulness should have taught us otherwise, but still we fail to heed Jesus' admonition:

> "Remain in me, and I will remain in you. No branch can bear fruit by itself; it must remain in the vine. Neither can you bear fruit unless you remain in me.
>
> "I am the vine; you are the branches. If a man remains in me and I in him, he will bear much fruit; apart from me

you can do nothing. If anyone does not remain in me, he is like a branch that is thrown away and withers; such branches are picked up, thrown into the fire and burned. If you remain in me and my words remain in you, ask whatever you wish, and it will be given you. This is to my Father's glory, that you bear much fruit, showing yourselves to be my disciples" (John 15:4-8).

Whatever you need to do in order to have time with God—do it! No longer allow yourself the excuses, rationalizations and lack of discipline that have kept you from being near to your Father in heaven. If Jesus needed quiet time with his Father, how much more do we?

Chapter 3

TIME AWAY

Time away from our usual routine and environment is essential in developing intimacy with God. We can see this from the examples of great men and women of the Bible, but once again, it is the practice of Jesus that most powerfully beckons us. Consider these examples from his life.

But Jesus often withdrew to lonely places and prayed (Luke 5:16).

One of those days Jesus went out to a mountainside to pray, and spent the night praying to God (Luke 6:12).

Once when Jesus was praying in private... (Luke 9:18).

Jesus...took Peter, John and James with him and went up onto a mountain to pray (Luke 9:28).

> One day Jesus was praying in a certain place. When he finished, one of his disciples said to him, "Lord, teach us to pray" (Luke 11:1).

> Jesus...withdrew again to a mountain by himself (John 6:15).

> Immediately Jesus made his disciples get into the boat and go on ahead of him to Bethsaida, while he dismissed the crowd. After leaving them, he went up on a mountainside to pray.
> When evening came, the boat was in the middle of the lake, and he was alone on land (Mark 6:45-47).

> Then, because so many people were coming and going that they did not even have a chance to eat, he said to them, "Come with me by yourselves to a quiet place and get some rest" (Mark 6:31).

I am amazed at how much time Jesus spent alone. Considering the vastness of his accomplishments in leading people, it is more striking still. How could we read the story of Jesus' life and miss it? In realizing this, we discover much of the secret of his greatness, his power in leading others and his uniquely close relationship with God. It was simply a matter of time—time spent alone, time spent in large amounts and time spent in lonely places without interruptions and distractions.

Have you ever spent a whole day completely away from people, all alone with the Lord? Have you ever spent an entire night in prayer, study and meditation? Have you ever gone away overnight on a personal retreat—solely for the purpose of drawing near to God?

Some of us have been disciples for years and have never done anything like this. And we wonder why we are stale, unmotivated, joyless and weary, and why we have not grown in our faith!

When my family lived in Boston, I went on a two-week fast, and on the last night I stayed up all night in prayer. Different brothers in the church joined me every other hour. It was an incredible time of growth for us all. I drew amazingly close to God, and the changes I made in my life and ministry because of the fast and the night of prayer helped to reshape my entire future.

Years later, before an important gathering of church leaders in Jerusalem, I took the better part of a day to pray. Several days before it began, I went away by myself and spent hours with God, praying for the conference, its leaders and participants and for my own heart to be attuned to God's message. I went to the conference in a better frame of mind and with a better attitude than I have ever had at an event like this—and as a result, I experienced a refreshing, heartening time of growth.

Last fall I gave a men's leadership group the challenge to spend a night alone outdoors in spiritual retreat. All of the men came back changed and inspired.

Many shared how it took them a while to detach from the world and unwind, but that as they did, they were able to pray, think and commune with God on an entirely different level. All of them promised themselves to make such personal retreats a regular part of their lives. I would challenge you to take out your calendar and plan such a time as soon as possible.

I will always treasure the memory of my own night away. I decided to sleep out in the open. After spending time in prayer, I turned in early. The sky was a sparkling tapestry of stars and the cool autumn wind sang soothingly through the pine trees overhead. I woke occasionally during the night, only to see the stars and hear the wind as it gently curled the waves against the lakeshore.

I arose before daylight and went down by the lake to read and pray and to watch the sun rise. I sang, I smiled, I cried and I prayed at length about everything on my heart. The sky slowly began to come alive with color and light. I kept awaiting the sun's appearance, but it seemed late in coming. I checked my watch, just to make sure the Lord had not slowed things down as he had done in Joshua's day. And while I was waiting, I realized something: *God just doesn't get in a hurry for anybody.* That was one of the most memorable of the many lessons I learned that night and morning. It may not seem like an earth-shaking revelation to you, but for me—anxious, in a hurry, tending to live for what is going to happen next, and always ready to help God move his timetable up to my liking—it was a lesson desperately needed.

A few of the other men reported some humorous moments. One brother, in the middle of the night, heard a *thump, thump, thump* coming toward his tent. Trying to be a fearless, mighty man of God, he attempted to ignore it, but the sound only grew louder and ominously closer. Finally, with a blood-curdling war cry he charged out of his tent to confront the unwelcome intruder. He found himself face to face with a fearsome bullfrog trying to make his way across the campsite to the lake on the other side of the tent!

☯

I write this paragraph having just returned from six days and five nights spent alone in a remote country inn writing this book. I felt that to write a book of this nature, I needed to be in an especially relaxed frame of mind and especially close to the Lord. The retreat was an unforgettable, life-changing time. In addition to writing, I spent hours walking, thinking, studying, praying and enjoying fellowship with God. Not only did I write most of this book, but more importantly, I was spiritually and emotionally renewed.

As I write these words now, I am back at home, sitting at my desk in my study. A few minutes ago I was startled by the first telephone ring I had heard in six days! It is amazing how clearly you can think, how much you can learn and how close to God you can draw when you are away from the distractions and duties of life.

Perhaps your responsibilities will not allow for the extended time I was able to take, but it is time that we all get serious about making time to go away and be with God. What a great use this would be of some of our vacation days! It will not happen by accident, nor will our schedules just miraculously open up. You will have to plan it and decide to make it happen. And once you have done it, you will long for more and more time away, alone with God.

Chapter 4
TIME OUTDOORS

Do you realize that nearly all of the people we read about in the Bible spent most of their time outdoors? From Adam to Abraham to Moses to David to Jesus, the people of the Bible were men and women who spent much of their lifetimes in direct contact with the world God made.

Their experiences in nature profoundly shaped their view of God and through that, their relationship with him. Jesus' parables were largely inspired by all that he saw as he walked the roads and fields of Galilee. God took Abraham outside to give him the spectacular view of the star-studded evening sky to tell him how great would be the numbers of his descendants (Genesis 15:5). And it was with the grandeur of creation that God humbled the petulant pride of Job (Job 38:4-7).

But times and lifestyles have changed, at least for many modern disciples. There are those of us who rarely go outside, and if we do, we quickly enclose ourselves

in our automobile until we arrive at the next building
we enter. Others of us emerge from our apartments,
walk several blocks through city streets, board a crowded
subway, and exit several miles away, feeling lucky if we
saw a few trees or a beam of sunlight peeking from
behind a skyscraper. I am sure many of us reading this
book have never spent a night in anything less than the
sturdiest of structures—a tent would be a challenge, and
the open air would be unthinkable! Is it any wonder
that we have lost our sense of the greatness of God? Is it
hard to understand why we are so self-centered and
faithless—when we rarely take the time to be in God's
beautiful, majestic world?

As I write these words, I am sitting at a desk surrounded by glass walls on three sides. I have checked
into an inn out in the North Carolina countryside miles
away from my home so that I can work undisturbed.
Earlier today I went for a run on the country roads
through the beautiful, rolling farmland. I saw only one
car—the local mailman out making his rounds. I was
surrounded by green pastures, trees blowing in the cold
winter breeze and the sounds and smells of the lush
countryside. I felt contented, relaxed and peaceful. As I
ran, I praised God for creating such beauty and for let-
ting me be there to see it; but mostly, I just enjoyed the
sense of how big, wise and glorious a God who could
make such a world must be.

I urge you to get outdoors. For some, it will be easy—just walk outside and discover your own backyard! For others who live in urban areas, it may take more effort, but the rewards are too great to be missed. As Winston Churchill once observed, "The whole world is open with its treasures. The simplest objects have their beauty." Find the parks, trails and open spaces. Go away occasionally to the countryside just to recharge your emotions and to renew your vision of the greatness and majesty of God. For all of us, it means every day we need to open our eyes, listen with our ears and breathe in the fragrances of a world full of beauty.

When was the last time you took in a sunrise or sunset over the ocean or a lake? Or when did you last notice the changing cloud formations that pile up in the sky like castles? When did you last stop to notice the beautiful birds that fly all around us or pause to listen to their song? Did you stroll through the leaves this fall or walk in the forest during a winter snowfall, with the woods so quiet you could hear the flakes as they gently fell to earth? Have you taken the time to look at the flowers of spring, to gaze deeply into one small blossom and be amazed at the rich, delicate colors that man could never produce? Have you stopped to watch the fearsome majesty of a thunderstorm, the power of the thunder and lightning? Have you gone out at night, away from the city lights, gotten outdoors and stood in awe of the sparkling stars and seemingly endless universe?

When you do, you will be closer to God. He will speak to you. He will speak to you as he spoke to Abraham when he showed him the stars. He will commune with you as he did with Jesus as they spent nights and days alone together, in precious respite from the demands of a selfish and unseeing world. He will speak to you as he did to a young shepherd boy alone on the hills of Bethlehem who was so moved by the vision of God in his world that he took up his harp and sang his heart out with praise:

> The heavens declare the glory of God;
> > the skies proclaim the work of his hands.
> Day after day they pour forth speech;
> > night after night they display knowledge.
> There is no speech or language
> > where their voice is not heard.
> Their voice goes out into all the earth,
> > their words to the ends of the world.
> (Psalm 19:1-4)

> Those living far away fear your wonders;
> > where morning dawns and evening fades
> > you call forth songs of joy.

> You care for the land and water it;
> > you enrich it abundantly.

The streams of God are filled with water
    to provide the people with grain,
    for so you have ordained it.
You drench its furrows
    and level its ridges;
you soften it with showers
    and bless its crops.
You crown the year with your bounty,
    and your carts overflow with abundance.
The grasslands of the desert overflow;
    the hills are clothed with gladness.
The meadows are covered with flocks
    and the valleys are mantled with grain;
    they shout for joy and sing
(Psalm 65:8b-13).

Time outside with God is just what many of us need, and nothing else will suffice. It's really not that complicated: The indefinable ache in your heart, the nameless loneliness you feel, may be nothing more than the need to go outside, out under the canopy of the heavens, and be alone with God.

Chapter 5

TIMES OF FASTING

The practice of fasting permeates the Scriptures. The examples are so numerous as to defy listing here, but several salient ones will help us see the frequency of this practice among those who have walked closely with God:

- *Moses* fasted for forty days as he received the Law (Exodus 34:28).
- *David* fasted for the life of his newborn child (2 Samuel 12:15-22).
- *King Jehoshaphat* of Judah declared a national fast under a time of military emergency (2 Chronicles 20).
- *Queen Esther* called for God's people to fast when they were threatened with extermination (Esther 4).
- *Daniel* fasted to confess his sin and the sin of God's people (Daniel 9).

- *Nehemiah* fasted when he heard of the deplorable condition of the remnant in Jerusalem (Nehemiah 1).
- *Jesus* fasted for forty days at the outset of his ministry (Matthew 4:2).
- *The Antioch church leaders* fasted and worshiped, as they sought God's blessing upon their missionary efforts (Acts 13:1-3).
- *Paul and Barnabas* dedicated newly appointed church elders to God with prayer and fasting (Acts 14:23-24).

There are no detailed instructions given in the Bible on how to fast. We are, however, given many examples of those who did and are often told the results of their fasts. Jesus declared that fasting was not a feature of the group that followed him during his earthly ministry, but it would be practiced by his future disciples (Luke 5:33-35). He warned of fasting merely for appearance and assumed that fasting would be a part of a believer's life (Matthew 6:16-18, Luke 18:9-14). Jesus and the Old Testament prophets warned that fasting in and of itself is of no benefit if it does not result in a righteous life or is not motivated by a righteous heart (Isaiah 58:3-6, Jeremiah 14:12).

Should we fast today? The examples of saints in both the Old and New Testament and the example and teaching of Jesus combine to give us an overwhelming "Yes" to that question. With this conviction established, let us return to gain a deeper understanding of this oft-neglected, oft-misunderstood spiritual discipline.

What is fasting? It is primarily associated with voluntary abstinence from food in order to draw near to God. The longest fasts of which we have record are those of Moses and Jesus. Most fasts were probably much shorter, closer to a day or several days in duration.

When we fast, I believe we are left to make our own decisions as to what will most encourage our drawing near to God. Not eating is the most obvious, and perhaps not drinking as well. (I would not recommend imitation of Moses' forty days without water—I think he had a supernatural life-support system up on that mountain!) In my own times of fasting I have found that abstaining from solid food and only allowing myself water or other liquids (juices) was of the greatest benefit. It is wise to decide in advance how long the fast is to go. It is also wise to begin with shorter fasts of one or two days if we have never fasted before. Some people have extreme or severe reactions to fasting and should proceed with caution. Let common sense prevail. If you have recently been ill, you should wait until you are fully recovered. If you are taking some sort of medication, you should read the instructions carefully and consult with your physician. If you now or in the past have struggled with anorexia or bulimia, you should not abstain from food but find other ways to fast. A final practical word: Do not indulge in a large meal immediately after a fast—too much food, too soon can be a painful shock to the system!

What are some other fasts we can embark upon? I have heard of many types of fasts by different disciples: fasts from movies, from sports, from television, from newspapers and magazines and from certain types of food (i.e. meats, desserts, alcohol; see Daniel 1:8-16). One of the most helpful fasts I have ever experienced was one recommended to me by my friend and discipler Steve Sapp. For one month he embarked upon a "world fast" in which he abstained from all sorts of worldly influences: television, newspapers, radio, movies and any type of reading that was not directly spiritual. He was so encouraged by his fast that I undertook a form of it myself for a month. The results were amazing! I was much more spiritually focused and alert; I accomplished an incredible amount of work; I was more effective in leading the church and vastly increased my overall spiritual impact. I highly recommend the "world fast," especially when you have not been spiritually sharp.

Why do we fast? Perhaps a simple list would be the most helpful way to consider the reasons:

- To humble ourselves before God and to show our dependence on him.
- To devote more time and focus to our spiritual lives. The time we would have spent eating or preparing food can be used in prayer and Bible study. Also, each time we remember that we are not eating (which can be a frequent recollection, especially at the beginning of a fast!) may serve to remind us of why we are fasting and thus to better focus our wandering thoughts.
- To ask for God's guidance as we face important decisions.
- To ask for God's help in a crisis.
- To ask for God's help in a time of temptation or trial.
- To ask for God's help in overcoming spiritual dullness and numbness.
- To overcome a time of spiritual lukewarmness or loss of our first love.
- To help us rebuild our relationship with God, if we have fallen away or have sinned grievously.
- To have a special, focused time of prayer weekly or monthly (i.e. for world missions, the conversion of our families, etc.).

- To pray about some particular need in the church or as a means of group repentance (i.e. church leaders may call for a collective fast).
- To express gratitude and thanksgiving for a remarkable blessing, answered prayer or spiritual victory.
- To ask God for a breakthrough in sharing our faith or for the change of heart of a lost person.
- To bring about a breakthrough when we feel we have reached a spiritual plateau and need to draw on deeper reservoirs of spiritual power to accomplish needed changes in our lives.

Fasting has been immensely beneficial in my walk with God. I would not be who I am without it, nor could I have made many of the desperately needed changes in my character that seemed impossible. There have been times when I felt overwhelmed with problems or uncertain about what direction to take, and fasting provided the closer fellowship and dependency upon God that brought me through victoriously. Often it was a few days spent in fasting that brought me out of a time of spiritual lethargy. I am convinced that in the various churches I have lead that times of fasting have taken those congregations to a more powerful impact and greater spirituality.

Wherever you may be spiritually, fasting will make a wonderful difference in your life, and it may be just what you need to take you to a new level of closeness and intimacy in your walk with God.

Chapter 6
ALL THE TIME

To be real, a relationship must be an all-the-time thing, not a sometime thing. Some of us are probably thinking right about now that our relationship with God is totally dependent upon or confined to the special times like quiet times, times away or times of fasting. To think this way is to compartmentalize our walk with God, and such an attitude will do immense harm to our relationship with him. This is why many of us struggle and are inconsistent in our walk with God: We feel that unless we are in some special place or that it is some special time, we cannot be close to God.

God wants to be close to us at all times, not just during special occasions. Jesus said, "I am with you always, to the very end of the age" (Matthew 28:20). That means that throughout the course of our days, whether we are isolated and alone with God or going about our everyday affairs, Jesus is with us. Paul tells us that we should "pray continually" (1 Thessalonians 5:17).

Obviously, he does not mean that we are to cease all normal activities and spend all of our time in prayer but that we should be continually in tune with God and in a prayerful spirit no matter what we are doing.

Do not confine your relationship with God to having great quiet times. As a matter of fact, your relationship with God does not depend on how you feel after you have had a quiet time, or even if you missed having one that day. I am not saying that we should not strive for consistency in our daily devotions with God, but I am saying that our walk with him is much greater than what we do in those special hours. We should learn to cultivate a sense of the presence of God no matter where we are or what we are doing. We should learn to pray short prayers as we go about our daily business and to pause at moments throughout the day to remember the Lord and consider thoughts from his word.

If we do not learn to do this, we will be very insecure and legalistic in our walk with God, and our entire day can be ruined by a short, flat or missed quiet time.

Learn to get up from your time of prayer and Bible study and walk with God all day long. If you have had the privilege of sharing a "mountaintop" time with God away, overnight or out of doors, do not leave God out there in the wilderness; bring him back with you into the city!

I am reminded of an incident in Nehemiah's life that illustrates this. Nehemiah had prayed, wept and fasted for days concerning the sad condition of the remnant of Jerusalem. He asked God to forgive him and his people, and he prayed fervently for their deliverance. After he finished his time of prayer, he went about his normal duties as wine steward for King Artaxerxes. The king noticed Nehemiah's downcast appearance and asked him what was troubling him. Nehemiah, in recounting the story, says "then I prayed to the God of heaven" (Nehemiah 2:4b). In spite of all the days of praying he had done earlier, Nehemiah prayed again just before opening his mouth to respond to the king's question. Now, *that* is an "all the time" relationship with God! Nehemiah brought the Lord with him out of his period of days of fasting and into his everyday working world where the opportunities to serve God were real. And though his prayer was offered in only an instant, in that moment he once again sought the help and guidance of his God.

∞

I would urge you to in no way slacken your efforts to have daily times alone with God and special times away with him that enable you to draw especially near to him. But those moments can never replace the ongoing, daily walk and closeness that you should have with God all the time. Both are needed and one should help the other. Let us resolve that wherever we are and whatever we are doing, we will be close to God "all the time."

PART TWO

Listening to God

Chapter 7

A LOVE AFFAIR
WITH THE WORD

I have read many great books, and some of them I
have reread many times. Most of those are spiritual books
that have taught me the essential truths about God and
his word. But there is one book to which I have returned countless times, and which I read every day of
my life. That book is, of course, the Bible.

I have tried to plumb to its deepest depth—and I
have never touched bottom. I have attempted to scale
to its heights, and at times have felt myself breathless in
the ascent—but I have never reached its summit. I have
ranged throughout its pages, seeking to find the limits
of its wisdom and knowledge, but in the efforts of a
lifetime I have only begun to discover the uncharted
wonders of its scope.

I have read passages for years, only to one day read
them again and realize that there was so much more

there than I had gleaned before. "This time I get it; this time I fully understand," I have said to myself as I studied a passage, or sought to understand the ways of God as revealed in a story in the Scriptures. But I have then heard someone else share an insight, or I have come back to read it later and have exclaimed, "Why didn't I see that before?!"

Such is the greatness of the Bible. What other book even comes close? Novelists and their works come and go. The poets rise and fall. Even great spiritual books can fade or become outdated. But the Bible continues to shine forth majestically despite the passing of years by the hundreds and thousands. In every culture and country, its message, when preached faithfully by righteous people, brings in converts in droves.

Why do we allow our Bibles to lay unopened or to be read casually? How can we who were saved by its message neglect it afterward?

David says that the godly person should delight in and meditate upon the Word (Psalm 1:2). The writer of Psalm 119 says that we should not neglect the law (word) of God (v16). He begs God to open his eyes to see its wonders (v18) and proclaims that when he fell in the dust, discouraged, that it was the Word that revived him (v25). And later in his psalm he declares his passionate love for the word (v97).

How about you? Do you have a love affair with your Bible? If you could have an entire day to read your Bible, would the prospect excite you, or would it be an onerous, unpleasant duty?

∞

We cannot be close to God without listening to him. We cannot listen to him without spending time in the Bible. And we cannot love God unless we love spending time in his word.

Chapter 8

EXCITING PERSONAL BIBLE STUDY

Think back and remember when you studied the Bible to become a disciple. Recall the excitement you felt as you read the Bible for the first time, or for the first time with any real understanding of its message. The words seemed to leap off the page. They struck deep into your heart with piercing conviction; they enlightened you with blazing insight; and they inspired you with new visions of possibility. As you learned, you made decisions, and so learned more. Ideas, thoughts, insights seemed to get in the way of one another as they came flooding into your mind from the pages of the Scriptures. You could hardly bear to put your Bible down, so enthralled you were with the great message you were learning.

What has happened to those days? What has happened to those experiences? When was the last time you had an exciting discovery in your personal Bible study? When was the last time you regretted having to close your Bible and go on with the activities of your day? When was the last time you pushed yourself for ways to find more time to spend in studying the Word? When was the last time, through your own wrestling with the Scriptures, you studied yourself out of a period of discouragement, a bad attitude, a sin or some other problem you faced?

If these experiences are in your distant past or have rarely or never happened in your life, you need to realize that you are not doing well spiritually. You are easy prey for Satan. You are still immature. You have not grown beyond your spiritual infancy, and have ceased growing as a disciple.

We have our excuses and rationalizations. We think that the days of excitement are for young Christians— we think being "mature" means being dead and lifeless! We may have even seen other older Christians who are this way and assumed it is the fate of us all. Far from it! Consider Paul, who after many years in the Lord said,

> Not that I have already obtained all this, or have already been made perfect, but I press on to take hold of that for which Christ Jesus took hold of me. Brothers, I do not consider myself yet to have taken hold of it. But one thing I do: Forgetting what is behind and straining toward what is ahead, I press on toward the goal to win the prize for which God has called me heavenward in Christ Jesus.

All of us who are mature should take such a view of things. And if on some point you think differently, that too God will make clear to you. Only let us live up to what we have already attained (Philippians 3:12-16).

The only way to live like this is to have a deep, growing relationship with God, which means to continue to feed on his word.

Some of us have become lazy. We no longer put in the mental and spiritual effort to dig into the Scriptures, to search them out for new or deeper insights. We are satisfied with what we already know. We are content to be spoon-fed: to let our evangelist, elders or discipleship partners wrestle with the Scriptures (and with us!) to straighten us out, all because we will not make the effort to straighten ourselves out. Preaching from the pulpit, teaching in church meetings, learning from discipleship partners — all of these are great, and without them we perish—but many of us are content to be preached at, taught and discipled, and we fail to do our part. It seems we have forgotten that Jesus calls upon us to deny *ourselves* (Mark 8:34), and we expect everyone else in the kingdom to whip us into shape! That is a definition of immaturity and of laziness. We need to hear the solemn warning for older Christians issued in the book of Hebrews:

We have much to say about this, but it is hard to explain because you are slow to learn. In fact, though by this time you ought to be teachers, you need someone to teach you the elementary truths of God's word all over again. You need milk, not solid food! Anyone who lives on milk, being still an infant, is not acquainted with the teaching about righteousness. But solid food is for the mature, who by constant use have trained themselves to distinguish good from evil.

Therefore let us leave the elementary teachings about Christ and go on to maturity, not laying again the foundation of repentance from acts that lead to death, and of faith in God, instruction about baptisms, the laying on of hands, the resurrection of the dead, and eternal judgment. And God permitting, we will do so (Hebrews 5:11-6:3).

There is a need for us to train ourselves as disciples (1 Timothy 4:7, Hebrews 5:14), and this is precisely where many older disciples have faltered, and why they are not prospering spiritually. Absolutely essential to us "training ourselves" is getting back into God's word on our own. As a matter of fact, this may be the first step to take to a time of real spiritual renewal that is long overdue.

∞

Recommit yourself to spending time in God's word. Put your heart in it. Ask God to lead you to the right passages and to open your eyes with insight. As you read, seek to hear what the Holy Spirit wants to say to you. Remember the words spoken through Isaiah:

> "This is the one I esteem
> > he who is humble and contrite in spirit,
> > and trembles at my word" (Isaiah 66:2).

Humble yourself before the Word. Open yourself to it. When you do, it will come alive to you again, because it was never really the Word that lost its power, but you who lost your heart.

Chapter 9

KEEPING A JOURNAL

Early on in my Christian life I began keeping a notebook in which I recorded my daily thoughts, insights and goals. I cannot overemphasize the difference this practice has made for me and for countless other disciples. Here are some of the reasons:

It gives you a jump start for your Bible study every morning. I am amazed at how quickly I forget what I read. Often I have opened up my journal and have been astonished at how much I had already forgotten from the morning before. But, if it is all written down, fallible human memory does not have the power to undermine all the hard work already done!

When we use a journal, we can build on a thought or a theme. We may need to study and think about some subjects for many days (or weeks, or months!) before we begin to understand and believe them the way we should. A journal helps us to not be shallow students who impulsively flit from one idea to another without really learning anything.

A journal becomes a diary that reveals to us our spiritual progress. One of the most helpful ways I use my journal is in review. As I go back and read over several days of notes, I can then see my own patterns of thought and the patterns of temptation and struggle. I can also recall the victories I have had that I may have overlooked.

A journal keeps us focused on our goals and convictions. We often come under great conviction due to a sermon, a discipling time, some event in our lives or our study of the Word. But how soon we forget! Even a strong conviction can quickly lose its force when it is not repeatedly reviewed and remembered. Usually, something is a weakness for us because we are blinded to it by our sin and ignorance. Often we would rather forget about the challenging issues in our lives and focus on what comes easy to us. The same is true of decisions and goals. We are well-meaning but lack discipline, focus and determination in maintaining our resolve. A journal in which we have recorded our convictions, repentance and goals keeps those things before our eyes on a daily basis.

A journal becomes the seedbed of great inspiration and insight. I can look back at some of the most enlightening and enriching studies I have had and find in my journal the place where I first set out on the journey. Rarely did I realize that I was onto something or that God was about to move to give me greater insight, as I first recorded my thoughts. Often the words I wrote down seemed rather plain. But as I continued to write, think and put scriptures and thoughts together, things began to happen. At times, my pen could barely keep pace with the flow of new ideas that were being generated. Sometimes the experience lasted for days!

Let me offer some practical advice on how best to start and use your journal.

I recommend using a substantial notebook. If we rely on flimsy notepads or random scraps of paper, we become disorganized. I also urge that your notebook be reserved solely for this purpose. Without a notebook that is dedicated as my journal, I tend to lose the habit of taking notes during my Bible study, and my study degenerates as a result. Some may be able to incorporate their journal into their class notebooks from school, or into their daily planner. I find that this tends to bring too much of the outside world into my private time with God. I seem irresistibly drawn to a distracting trek into the other pages, or I simply feel the pull of my daily responsibilities beckoning me from their easily accessible location nearby. And, quite frankly, I do not want to chance losing my journal, with its important and private information, by taking it out of my home as I go about the business of my day.

I keep a small stack of adhesive notes in the front pocket of my journal. This helps me stay spiritually focused and yet be practically responsible; then, as I invariably remember some errand or responsibility that lies ahead of me, I can quickly note it for use later, without having to interrupt my quiet time. I also find that it is best to plan my day immediately following my quiet time. At that time I am most clear-minded and spiritually sharp. I have just finished praying about my day and its challenges and can do the best job of laying out my schedule, refreshed from my time with God.

Use your journal to write down and keep your goals before you. It is wise to read your goals daily until they are deeply impressed upon your heart. A journal is also a way to record your spiritual, emotional and mental condition. You can then go back and read how you have been doing and feeling over a period of time and make decisions about any necessary changes; or you can claim the victories God has been giving you!

∞

A journal is a wonderful way to train ourselves and to work out our salvation (1 Timothy 4:7-8, Philippians

2:12-13). If you are serious about growing in your walk with God, a journal can be the tool you need to take you to a new level of maturity. I would urge you to secure a notebook, place it on your bookshelf near your Bible, and use it every day!

Chapter 10

DECIDING WHAT TO STUDY

How do we decide what to study? The Bible is a large book, and there is more to learn than we seem capable of grasping in a lifetime. How do we make good decisions on what to study?

The best way I have found is by asking myself the following questions: *What is my greatest spiritual need right now?* and *In what do I most need to grow?* Here it might also be helpful to seek the advice of a discipleship partner or some other spiritual leader. Pray about your decision, asking God to make it clear what your focus needs to be. It is best to center upon spiritual needs rather than upon a mere desire for knowledge. God's purpose in us knowing anything is that it might help us to know him better and that it might transform us into the people he would have us be. There is nothing so exciting as the feeling of sitting down to study the Bible knowing that you are studying just what the Lord would have you hear! It is as if God himself is speaking to you from the pages of the Bible—and he is!

Here are some questions to ask yourself to help guide you to the right place:

Do I need to see Jesus?

If so, then read the Gospels. Matthew focuses on Jesus' teachings; Mark focuses on his deeds, John on his thoughts and Luke on his relationships with people.

Do I need to be more spiritual?

Study the Sermon on the Mount (Matthew 5-7), or do a topical study focusing on prayer or the heart.

Do I need more faith?

The approaches to this great subject are virtually endless: Study faith in the entire Bible, or focus on Jesus' teachings on faith, or Paul's. Study Hebrews 11, God's "hall of fame" of faith.

Do I need to learn to love others more?

Study love in the writings of a specific author like John, Peter or Paul. Study all that Jesus said about love. Study 1 Corinthians 13. Study how John was transformed from the Son of Thunder to the Apostle of Love.

Do I need to be more grateful?

Study the Psalms. Study the beginnings of Paul's letters. Do a topical study of words like "thankful" or "thanksgiving," or study "praise."

Do I need to become evangelistic and fruitful?

Study John 15:1-17, or all of Jesus' parables having to do with fruit, growth, harvest, etc. (See Mark 4.) Study Jesus' example of evangelism and his different challenges to us about evangelizing. Look at the example of the early church in the book of Acts or all that Paul said about sharing our faith. Study out the subjects of boldness and courage.

Do I need to know God better?

Study God's personal interactions with some of the great Old Testament characters like Abraham or Moses. Read the Psalms.

Do I need greater assurance of my salvation?

Study the theme of grace, especially in the writings of Paul. Study the concept of the greatness of our salvation in the book of Hebrews.

Do I need to learn how to lead?

Study the great leaders like Moses, Joshua, Nehemiah and David. Study the letters of Paul to the young leaders Timothy and Titus. In my early years of ministry I studied and restudied those books and imagined that Paul was writing them to me personally. Every morning as I showered and dressed for work, I memorized 2 Timothy. I gained from this a great understanding of the heart of a young man in the kingdom (and a soggy Bible, as well!).

Do I need to be renewed and revived as an older disciple?

The book of Hebrews was written for this very purpose study it! Read Jesus' messages to the seven churches in Revelation 2-3. Study the lives of men and women of God as they aged in both the Old and New Testament.

Do I need a greater conviction of sin?

Study the account of David's sin and its consequences in 2 Samuel 11-18. Study the Ten Commandments, the acts of the sinful nature of Galatians 5 and similar lists in Colossians 3 and Ephesians 4-5. Reflect upon what Jesus said about sin in the Sermon on the Mount and in Mark 7:20-21.

Do I need to repent of sin?

Study David's psalms of repentance (32, 38, 51 and others). Study Paul's (Saul's) repentance, as recorded in Acts. Study the attitude of worldly versus godly sorrow in 2 Corinthians 7:8-11 and James' powerful call to repentance in James 3 and 4. I would particularly encourage a study of how we should repent quickly and not be continually burdened by guilt once we have repented (Psalm 51 will be especially helpful here).

Do I need a deeper prayer life?

Look at the prayers of Moses, Abraham, Nehemiah, Daniel and other heroes of the Old Testament. Study the prayer life of Jesus. Study the prayers of Paul, as found throughout his letters.

Do I need help as a husband, wife or parent?

Study Proverbs 31:10-31, Ephesians 5:21-6:4, Colossians 3:18-21, 1 Peter 3:1-7 and the examples of Eli and of David in 2 Samuel.

Do I need help in dealing with suffering or persecution?

Read what Jesus said about it (i.e. the Sermon on the Mount and John 15:18-27). Read about the early church's persecutions in Acts or what Peter and Paul shared about it in their letters.

Do I need inspiration and encouragement?

Read the book of Joshua; study the life of Peter. Study the great battles of the Old Testament. Study the courageous deeds of prophets like Elijah, Elisha and

Daniel. Learn from the amazing example of Joseph in Genesis (chapters 37-50).

Am I not sure what I need?

Read the letters of Paul, Peter and John in the New Testament or read the Gospels.

I would also encourage you to commit passages of the Bible to memory. When you are given verses to memorize in a Bible class, do so enthusiastically. Also, select verses that are of special encouragement to you, and memorize them. Memorize your favorite psalms or paragraphs. I have already shared that I, as a young minister, memorized 2 Timothy. I recently committed to memory Isaiah 40—one of my favorite chapters in all of the Bible. What a feeling of accomplishment, and how helpful it has been to me in my walk with God! Memorizing passages like this (especially the psalms) is of incredible benefit in our prayer lives and in times of discouragement.

∞

Pray, think and obtain advice. Decide what to study, and dig in, knowing that God will richly bless your efforts!

Chapter 11

HOW TO STUDY

You want to have enriching, life-changing Bible study. How do you go about it? Many disciples are frustrated in their attempts to study the Bible on their own. They thumb through their Bibles, read a few passages, don't get much out of it and then assume that there just isn't much there for them.

How wrong this thinking is, and how unfortunate is your experience! God intends every disciple to delight in his word and to discover its wonders (Psalms 119:18). This can be, and must become, your personal experience if you are to mature as a disciple and walk closely with the Lord.

Let me suggest several approaches that can get you started:

Study one book of the Bible. Focus for a period of time on one book or on one of the New Testament letters. Read it through in its entirety, preferably in one sitting. Get a feel for what the Holy Spirit is saying in the book as a whole. Make a simple outline. Write down the main characters and events. Then in smaller portions study and restudy the book until it begins to open up to you. This usually takes awhile, and most of us lose patience before we begin to "get it." We marvel at those who seem to have greater insight than we do, and we feel we must lack some special gift of understanding. What we lack is prayerful, patient devotion to the Word! In many of my personal studies (see Chapter 13), I had to keep working, reading, thinking and praying for days (or even weeks!) before I had a breakthrough of insight that opened the book up to me. Relationships take time to build. In "building a relationship" with a particular book, stay with it until the two of you become friends!

Study a section of a book. Find a section of several chapters that comprise a story or unified thought, and tackle it. The Sermon on the Mount (Matthew 5-7) can keep you busy for a while! Jesus and the apostles in the upper room (John 13-17) brings you into the time when Jesus shared his last, most intimate and important teachings with his trusted disciples. Romans 5-8 tells us of the immense benefits of being justified by faith. There are many other such sections that can be effectively studied as a grouping of chapters.

Study one chapter of the Bible. Select a chapter or a psalm, and dig in. Use the same principles as in studying a book, but apply them to the shorter and more manageable study of a single chapter. You may find this a less daunting task, especially if you are a new student. Many chapters have such a strong message in and of themselves that they lend themselves readily to this approach. Some suggestions: 1 Corinthians 13, Isaiah 53, Psalm 23, Romans 12, Hebrews 11, Proverbs 31:10-31 (especially for women), Joshua 1.

Study one section or paragraph. Choose a smaller portion of Scripture that jumps out at you. Spend several days absorbing the message of it. Some suggestions: Philippians 2:1-11, 2 Timothy 2:1-7, Ephesians 3:14-21, 2 Peter 1: 5-9, Isaiah 40:27-31.

Study one verse. Sometimes in one sentence we have a statement of such depth, importance and profundity that it deserves prolonged and intense scrutiny. Oftentimes we breeze by these great lines, not allowing their powerful messages to sink in. Prolonged reflection and study of a single verse like this can be life-changing. Study the sentence. Break it down phrase by phrase, word by word. Compare it to similar statements elsewhere in the Bible. Look up the meaning of each word in a standard dictionary and in a Bible dictionary. Some suggestions: John 14:6, Matthew 17:20, Philippians 4:13, Romans 8:1, 1 John 4:19, James 1:19-20, Proverbs 3:5-6.

Study one topic. Decide upon a biblical subject or theme you want to understand and master, then research it throughout the Scriptures. This will give you a broad knowledge of a subject and will help you see how the whole Bible fits together. For this you will need a topical or chain-reference Bible, a concordance, or a computer word search program. As helpful as these tools are, challenge yourself to think on your own of every passage that relates to your theme. Some suggestions: love, grace, obedience, repentance, the heart, the Holy Spirit, angels, prayer, the "one another" passages, evangelism, holiness...the list is exciting and long!

Study one character. The Bible is the story of God interacting with very real people. Some of the most exciting, enlightening studies I have done are character studies. In them I have discovered those characters who have my strengths and weaknesses and have made them my lifetime friends. Some of my favorites are Joseph, David, Jonathan, Peter and Timothy. Study the great, well-known men and women like Moses, Abraham, Sarah, Rebekah, Rachel, Paul, John and Mary. Study the lesser known like Abigail, Stephen, Barnabas, Caleb and Priscilla and Aquila. Study those in your particular age group. (For example my sons studied "teenagers of the Bible" and loved it!) Study the weak and failing such as Aaron, Saul (Israel's first king), Absalom and Judas. You will be amazed, encouraged, warned and informed— and you will see how God relates to you and wants to work more in your life. Here again, it is helpful to use a concordance or study Bible. Also of help are different books written about Bible characters. But, as always, don't be lazy—do the work of study for yourself!

∽

Use your imagination. Work hard and be patient. Take notes and review them each day. Pray for insight. You will find that your Bible begins to come alive to you as the Spirit rewards your efforts with his enlightenment and that you draw closer to God as you listen to the message of his word.

Chapter 12

SEVEN QUESTIONS TO ASK

When I was a young disciple, I read a book in which the author shared seven questions to ask yourself as you study the Scriptures.* I found them useful then, and I find them useful now. If you are having difficulty finding any treasure in your personal Bible study, I highly recommend this approach.

1. Is there a promise to claim?

Is there a promise in this verse? If so, what is it? Is it possible for God to lie about his promises? What are the conditions and premises of the promise? Have I been claiming this promise, or is it going unfulfilled in my life?

2. Is there a command to obey?

Is there something God expects me to do? Have I been doing it? Have I been consistent? How can I get started?

* Paul Little, *How to Give Away Your Faith* (Downer's Grove, Illinois: Intervarsity Press) 1966, 126-127.

3. Is there a sin to avoid?

Is there a sin God is telling me to forsake? Am I guilty of this sin? When? How? To whom do I need to confess? How can I avoid this sin?

4. Is there a teaching about God, Jesus, the Holy Spirit or other Bible subjects that I need to believe?

Much of what we read in the Bible is informative: We learn about the nature of God, the personality of Jesus, the work of the Holy Spirit, the nature of people and the world around us, etc. It is vital for us to absorb the truths of God on whatever subject the Bible addresses.

5. Is there an example to follow or avoid?

The Bible tells the stories of people with whom God was involved. There are many inspiring examples to imitate. Find your Bible hero and learn from his or her life! There are sobering stories of how some of the great people fell. There are also stories of evil people and how they rebelled against God and God's word. Learn from these examples, and record what your response should be.

6. Is there a difficulty to explore?

We will read many passages in the Bible that challenge our thinking.

"As the heavens are higher than the earth,
     so are my ways higher than your ways and my
     thoughts than your thoughts" (Isaiah 55:9).

Sometimes we are thrown by a Bible difficulty. We struggle to understand, and perhaps even find ourselves doubting the truth of what we have read. Then we become fearful and guilty, and our faith is weakened. Others of us just overlook difficult passages and do not try to understand that which challenges our faith, understanding or intellect.

First, we must not let difficulties throw us, but instead inspire us to think, study, read and ask questions. God is trustworthy and his word remains true, even though there is a passage with which we may struggle. Second, we must realize that there are some things that are difficult because the Bible has not said much about them, or because our limited human minds have difficulty grasping them. Even the inspired apostle Peter, when confronted by some of Paul's challenging subject matter said:

Bear in mind that our Lord's patience means salvation, just as our dear brother Paul also wrote you with the wisdom that God gave him. He writes the same way in all his letters, speaking in them of these matters. His letters contain some things that are hard to understand, which

ignorant and unstable people distort, as they do the other
Scriptures, to their own destruction (2 Peter 3:15-16).

Third, remember to interpret obscure or difficult passages in the light of clearer ones. Start with the verses
that speak clearly to a subject before you tackle a statement that is more complex.

Last, we must remember to not focus upon lesser
matters but to instead build our faith on that which is
plain and obvious. While it is a good thing to have curi-
osity and explore challenging subjects, it is not wise to
become speculative. Given time and further study, difficulties usually resolve themselves and apparent contra-
dictions turn out to be harmonious.

7. Is there something in the passage I need to pray about today?

Your Bible study should give you plenty of spiritual
focus for your time of prayer. If God has spoken to you
through the Scriptures, don't change the subject! Pray in
thankfulness for the promises, with confession of any
sin, in surrender to any command—let your Bible study
make your prayer life even more powerful and relevant.

Chapter 13

BIBLE STUDIES THAT CHANGED MY LIFE

There are countless ways that my personal study of the Bible has changed my life, and I thought I would share some of them with you.

The earliest study I can recall that helped me was the one I did as I was seeking to become a disciple. I was a sophomore in college, during a time of great unrest on campus. College campuses are generally places of skepticism and resistance to authority, and mine (The University of Florida) seemed unusually so at the time. I came in contact with the campus ministry there and was both afraid of and inspired by what I saw and heard. I immediately had to confront my doubts. I doubted everything—God, the Bible, the miracles and Jesus being the Son of God. I turned to the Bible for answers, especially to the Gospel of John.

I read it over and over again, listening to Jesus' words and hearing his call to faith. I studied the "signs" he gave and the testimony of his own words and of the words of those who believed in him. Slowly and surely, my faith began to grow, until one day I decided to put my full trust in Jesus and give him my life.

In the months immediately following my conversion, I devoured the letters of Paul. Since so many of them were written to young churches, I felt as though they were personally addressed to me. I established myself in the basics of the Gospel message: grace, forgiveness, justification by faith, righteous living and the need for close friendships in the church.

A few years later I once again had a life-changing encounter with the Gospel of John. I particularly focused on chapters 13-17. I was fascinated by the incredible promises of fruitfulness, of the indwelling Spirit and of the power of prayer. I was amazed at the kind of intimacy Jesus promised that his followers were to have with him. Perhaps even more than what I learned was the excitement of learning itself—of seeing the Bible come alive every day as I read for longer and longer periods of time. I filled up the margins of my four-translation Bible with notes. Then I filled up the pages of my journal with notes. It seemed as if I could not write fast enough to record all that I was learning. As a mature disciple today, I still rest upon the incredible truths I gained in those exciting months, and I often go back to John's gospel to be reminded of and renewed in them, and to learn more. And as an evangelist, I continue to preach those crucial concepts I learned so many years ago.

As a young ministry intern and leader, I took Paul's letters to Timothy and Titus as my own. I imagined what it would have been like to be Timothy and to receive a letter from the great apostle. I imagined that they were written to me. I strove to make them a part of my very soul, as I worked under the lead evangelist in the church. The teachings of those letters inspired me and called me to a level of commitment, sacrifice, courage and humility that I had never realized was possible.

As I matured, I discovered David and the Psalms. David became, next to Jesus, my greatest Bible hero. I identified with him as he strove to follow God as a young man. I was inspired beyond comprehension by his humble but courageous confrontation with Goliath. And, as I began to face the challenges of dealing with conflict within the kingdom and of responding to those who let me down, David's pure-hearted attitude toward his unfair treatment by Saul inspired me to never fall away. I saw in Jonathan the model of loyal friendship and the willingness to humbly step aside so that another man could do greater things than I. I saw in Saul and Absalom the roots of bitterness that I never wanted to allow to grow in my own heart. And I learned in reading the Psalms how to become real with God and how to let my heart sing for joy and pour out its sorrows. I began to pray the Psalms for myself, and in so doing I was taken to a level of intimacy with God that I had never known existed.

After a time of failure and struggle in the ministry, my family and I moved to Boston. There, we worked to regain our vision and to learn how to build churches. I found myself discouraged because of my past failures, wondering if God could ever use me again. For months I studied Isaiah 40-66 and gradually felt my soul come alive with hope. I saw that if God's love could be so tender and forgiving for his rebellious children of Israel, then how much more for me? I began to believe that God's grace was indeed greater than my sin and that I could be restored—and become even more effective than I had dreamed in the past.

As I entered into my forties, I faced the challenges of middle age—the cynicism, anger, loss of idealism and loss of fire that tempts and destroys so many in those crucial years. I discovered a book in the Bible that transformed my thinking about life and about those years: the book of Ecclesiastes. In it I saw a man who had lost his ideals as he faced a cruel world of vanity and selfishness, a world that for a time robbed him of the joy of life. I learned that I could see the world as it is without losing my innocent faith in God or losing the ability to enjoy the life God has given me in his kingdom.

My greatest and most beloved study of them all is Jesus. In all the years of believing, serving, following, striving, repenting and overcoming, he remains the greatest subject in the Bible. I never tire of reading about his example, hearing his words, marveling at his poise, being convicted and inspired by his perfectly balanced character. Time after time when my well runs dry, I return to the pages where he is found that I may be once again reminded of why I do everything I do.

Find your own life-changing studies. Ask God to lead you to them. Study, think, pray and study some more. And one day you will look back with gratitude and joy at a time of listening to God and his word that forever changed your life.

PART THREE

Speaking to God

Chapter 14
THE PATTERN

What are we to pray about and in what order? How can we organize our thoughts and prayers in such a way that we know we are speaking to God about what he would have us speak? God has not left such crucial issues to guesswork. He has left us a divine pattern, and if we learn to follow it, our prayer lives will attain heights we never dreamed possible.

Like many people, I struggled with the problem of a wandering mind in prayer. I also felt that oftentimes I was only praying about a limited number of subjects. It was then that I discovered the teachings of Jesus on the matter, put them into practice, and went on to a new level of closeness with God.

We call it "The Lord's Prayer," and in one sense it is, because the Lord gave it to us. But in another sense it should be called "The Disciple's Prayer," because the Lord taught disciples to pray it and because there was one part Jesus never had to pray: the request for forgiveness.

It is found in Matthew 6:9-13, and I would urge that above all other scriptures you study on the subject of prayer, that you focus on understanding these verses. Also study the context around them to gain a full appreciation of Jesus' attitudes about the essence of prayer. We will briefly study each phrase of this immortal teaching, but first let us make these observations:

This is a pattern of prayer, and not a formula. It was never meant to be recited in rote fashion—either once or many times. (See the verses immediately preceding it for Jesus' rebuke of this practice!) Instead, it was taught as a model of the full scope and subject matter we should address in our conversations with God. The different subjects should be regarded as that: as subjects to pray about. However, we should not feel that this is the only way to pray nor the only order in which to pray. Prayer is much too dynamic a thing to be reduced to one order. Instead, I would suggest that we should make use of this prayer as a manner of praying, without feeling that we are displeasing to God if we vary from it.

Praying the Lord's Prayer may at first seem awkward. Do not allow that feeling to discourage you. It seemed awkward for me, too, but I stuck with it and now feel a bit uncomfortable when I digress from it!

Be prepared to spend more time in prayer when you use this prayer. Many of us can be amazed at the amount of time other disciples invest in one prayer session. "How can you go so long?" we ask. "I run out of things to pray about in a few minutes. Aren't you just repeating yourself?" Far from creating the mindless repetition that Jesus rebuked in Matthew 6:7, praying the Lord's Prayer instead encourages personal prayer that covers a wider range of subjects, thus the possibility of more time spent.

The structure of the prayer itself reveals the genius of God. The prayer begins as we praise God for his love and holiness. We then move to petition on behalf of the kingdom and God's will for our lives. Then we address our daily needs and sins. Next we center upon God's power to deliver us from sin and temptation and end our prayer once again focused on God's great dominion, power and glory. Do you see the wisdom of this? Our prayers are so often consumed with *us*—our needs, our feelings, our sins, our worries. God does not want us to neglect these concerns in prayer, but he wants us to be centered upon *him*—his love, his holiness, his kingdom and his power to deliver us. So we begin by looking to God; then we deal with ourselves; and as we close, we once again focus on God. Pray this way, and see the incredible change this will make in your frame of mind during and after prayer. God's plan in the Lord's Prayer is amazing! I am convinced that Jesus used this pattern of prayer, and this is one reason he prayed for so long and came away with such amazing poise and peace in his heart afterwards.

Notice the use of the pronoun "us" throughout this prayer. Our prayers are to be personal, but not self-centered. That we will be in prayer for others is assumed throughout.

Now let us briefly examine each part of this great prayer, with the goal of learning to pray each phrase as a subject.

"Our Father..." Jesus radically changed the way we address God, because he changed the nature of the relationship. We are now no longer slaves, but sons and daughters! (Galatians 4:7). We are children approaching a willing, loving Father who is eager to be with us, to know us and be known by us. Though God is infinitely above us in wisdom, power and holiness, we can approach him with confidence because of the cross and the continually cleansing blood of Jesus. Our status before God has been permanently altered: We are now in his family and are beloved children.

Many disciples believe this about God, but still live in fear. Many of us carry a vague sense of guilt and condemnation in our hearts. We are afraid to believe that God is our Father—and that he really loves us. Or we believe he loves us in some distant way, but not in an intimate, affectionate way. We think that he may love

us, but he really doesn't *like* us that much! The Bible
teaches that God delights in us, that we are his trea-
sured possession, and that we now have a relationship,
not of servile fear, but of confident, affectionate love. I
would suggest you spend much time studying the verses
referenced at the end of this section, but even more, I
would urge you to thank God that they are true as you
begin your time of prayer—only then will you grasp
emotionally and *relationally* the great concept of the
fatherhood of God.

Verses to study:

> Psalms 16:3, 103:13-14, 147:11, 149:4
> Proverbs 3:12
> Isaiah 62:4, 65:19
> Zephaniah 3:12
> Romans 8:1, 15-16
> Galatians 3:26-4:7
> Ephesians 3:12
> Hebrews 10:19-23
> 1 John 3:19-20, 4:16-18

"In heaven..." God is in heaven! This is the place
where he dwells and where we long to be when we
die. God is there, in all his glory, surrounded by countless angels. Above all, he is there with Jesus, who sits at

his right hand to intercede on our behalf as our great high priest. We have the confidence to enter into the very throne room of God that we may speak to him. In prayer we must lift up our eyes and minds from our preoccupation with earthly things and gain a heavenly perspective. We will soon die and be with God in heaven—Paul said that he would rather have been there than here—and he had a joyful life here! When we think of heaven, we also need to praise God that his resources there are limitless, that he owns the earth and everything on it and all of the created universe and all the eternal glory of heaven, as well!

Verses to study:

Romans 8:22-25

Philippians 4:19

1 Peter 1:3-5

Revelation 4, 5, 7:9-17, 19:1-10, 21:1-4, 22

"Hallowed be your name." When the Bible uses the word "name" in the sense that it does here, it does so to sum up all the qualities and characteristics of the individual. For instance, when public officials act in the "name" of the law, they act on behalf of all that the law stands for, for all that it says and means. When Jesus refers to the "name" of our Father as "hallowed" or

holy, he means that we should recognize that God's character and being is holy, or set apart, above us and to be treated as holy. It means we should revere God and stand in awe of his perfection, beauty, might, wisdom and glory.

Prayer is not just asking God for something; it is worshiping him, and honoring him for all that he is. This is not a foolish thing to do, although it could seem so to us. It is not as if God were uncertain as to who he is and needs us to remind him! It is instead that we need to recognize who he is so that we might approach him with proper confidence ("Our Father") and reverence ("hallowed be your name").

"Your kingdom come." At the outset of his ministry Jesus proclaimed that the kingdom of God was near. Later he said that it would come with power in the lifetime of some of those who heard him preach (Mark 9:1). Between the time of his resurrection and ascension, he told some of his followers to wait in Jerusalem for the power from on high that the Father had promised (Luke 24:49). We find the promise of the kingdom's arrival fulfilled on the day of Pentecost as the apostles proclaim the death, burial and resurrection of the now-exalted Jesus. Three thousand responded and were baptized into Christ and into his kingdom, the church. So in what sense should we pray for the kingdom to come, since it already has?

The kingdom has not come to every nation, nor has it come to every person! There are untold millions who have never heard the true message of the Good News and others who have heard but have not yet accepted it. Jesus told us that the harvest was plentiful but that the workers were few and that we should therefore pray for the Lord of the harvest to send out workers (Matthew 9:37-38). Paul begged the churches to pray that God would open doors for him to preach and that he would have the courage to speak boldly and the wisdom to preach well (Ephesians 6:19-20, Colossians 4:3).

This is the time when we should plead for our lost friends and family, and for God to make us fruitful in his service. This is the time to pray for our evangelists, women's ministry leaders and other leaders in our local church and in churches around the world. This is the time to pray for God to move the hearts of leaders and governments to open their nations to the preaching of the Word. It is the time for us to request that God will raise up more leaders (workers) to be full-time in his service and for every member of God's kingdom to fulfill their part in seeking and saving the lost.

I would challenge you to pray for the salvation of your family and loved ones every day. I would urge you to daily pray for the leaders of your congregation and for your own opportunities to share your faith, that you would have the wise, loving heart for the lost that Jesus had. Let us pray that the kingdom will come!*

Verses to study:
Matthew 9:35-38
Ephesians 6:19-20
Colossians 4:2-6
2 Thessalonians 3:1-2

"Your will be done on earth as it is in heaven." Much of what God wants us to pray is to surrender our will to his—much of what we pray is just the opposite! The Lord's Prayer will help us to get our priorities straight: It places surrender to God at an early stage of our prayer. This will oftentimes result in a time of struggle in prayer, as we examine ourselves and surrender our will. Our attitude needs to be like that of David who asked God to search his heart and life and point out anything that was amiss (Psalm 139:23-24). It may be that there is a challenge or trial approaching that we would rather avoid, but that we must face with a surrendered life. It may be that, like Jesus, we will have to stay up all night and pray

---

*This line of the prayer very much goes with the next line ("Your will be done"). Most scholars see here an example of Hebrew parallelism. In other words the kingdom of God, in one sense, is wherever the will of God is being done. This is why Jesus would say that 'The kingdom of God is within you" (Luke 17:21). With that in mind we can still pray for the kingdom to come to our own lives. The word "kingdom" can also be translated "reign" or "rule." We may be in the kingdom, but as we will see in the next section, we need to always be submitting ourselves to the reign of God, and our prayer needs to be for God's rule to keep coming to our hearts and minds.

repeatedly until our heart is finally at rest, committed fully to doing the will of God, no matter how difficult (Matthew 26:36-44).

If you are wondering what to pray about in this area, read some of the commands of God and ask yourself if you are obeying them. If you are not, it is time to surrender, and the place to begin is in prayer. In the verses in Matthew referred to above, you will notice that Jesus never asked for strength to go to the cross, but only that he might surrender. I wonder if many of our prayers requesting strength should be replaced by prayers of surrender, knowing that if we are obedient, God's power is absolutely guaranteed!

Some decisions we face are matters of judgment rather than a clear case of obedience to a specific command. In these cases we need to pray for wisdom that we might "discern what is best" (Philippians 1:9-11) and that we might be given wisdom (James 1:5-8).

What keeps us from doing God's will? Besides our pride and rebellion, is it not our unbelief? We doubt that God has our best interests at heart. We think that he somehow takes delight in ruining our lives and robbing us of happiness. The cure for this attitude is to remember the rest of the phrase that we are discussing: that God's will be done on earth "as it is in heaven." Now, just what kind of place is heaven? The last time I checked, it was the happiest, most joyful place I ever heard of!

When we surrender our lives, we find our true joy. After we pray and say "your will be done," the power to obey is given, and the joy flows in!

Verses to study:
 1 John 5:3-5
 Acts 16:6-10
 1 Peter 4:1-2

"Give us today our daily bread." This is the time to bring before God our specific daily needs. Nothing is too big or too small for God. He is concerned about the details of our lives. As the Israelites learned to depend on God each day for manna in the desert, so we must depend on God daily for our spiritual and physical needs. I would suggest opening up your daily calendar or "to do" list and praying through every detail on it for the day, no matter how trivial it may seem.

Many of us are anxious and worried about our finances, schedule, health, studies—and yet we do not bring God into the picture. Jesus said that we could do nothing apart from God (John 15:5). It is our pride and unbelief that prevent us from trusting and praying as we should.

Verses to study:
 Exodus 16:1-32
 John 15:5

"Forgive us our debts, as we also have forgiven our debtors." Confession of sin must be an ongoing part of our relationship with God. Since we usually sin every day, we need to confess frequently. Hopefully, our sins will not be of such a magnitude as to destroy our walk with God, but all sin must be taken seriously and must be taken before the Lord in prayer.

Many disciples do not practice confession in their private prayers. This can result in a hardened heart and an increasing boldness in sin. It is best to confess sin quickly so that it will not separate us from God. Lack of proper confession can result in a vague sense of guilt, a condemning conscience. As a result, we may always be a bit insecure and self-conscious, and we may not feel comfortable or happy in our Christian lives. Others of us depend on sermons or discipling times to convict us and rarely do any soul-searching in prayer. Thus we remain forever immature, depending on others to do for us what we should be doing on our own before the Lord.

In our daily prayers we should always include a time of self-examination and confession. Some days we may not have much to confess. If so, thank God for his mercy and grace, and move on. Don't try to make up a sin just so you will have something to say! On the other hand, don't breeze by this time because it makes you uncomfortable. The way we are individually built emotionally and temperamentally will have much to do with our difficulties in this area and a healthy dose of self-knowledge will serve us well here.

Be specific in your confession. Confess any sinful word, thought or deed. If you need to ask another person's forgiveness, do so at your first opportunity. If you need help in conquering a particular sin, open up about it to your discipleship partner or some trusted spiritual leader.

This is also the time in which we extend forgiveness to others. This is the only part of the Lord's Prayer that Jesus elaborated upon (Matthew 6:14-15). Bitterness and unforgiveness are two of the deadliest spiritual killers. We cannot expect to be forgiven by God if we refuse to forgive those who have sinned against us. Search your heart, and if you find any unforgiveness, decide that you will forgive. Forgive as freely as you want God to forgive you, and you will be amazed at the burdens that are lifted from your heart as you pray!

Verses to study:
> Psalm 139:23-24
> Matthew 18:21-35
> Colossians 3:13
> James 5:16

"And lead us not into temptation, but deliver us from the evil one." Jesus set the example of taking his needs before the Father in prayer as he faced temptation. In Matthew 26:36-43 he anticipated Satan's attack and stayed up all night in agonizing prayer that he would overcome it. He challenged the sleeping disciples to wake up and pray that they might overcome the trials that were soon to come upon them (Matthew 26:41). We can see both the results of his prayer as he victoriously went to the cross, and of his disciples' failure to pray as their resolve crumbled under pressure.

What are your weaknesses? What are your besetting sins, those areas of sin to which you are most susceptible? Where is Satan focusing his attack in your life right now? He always has a plan, and he is always looking to exploit any moment when our guard is down. We must draw on God's power *before* Satan strikes. Many disciples who are being continually defeated in battles with sin have not taken their battles before the Lord. We should pray for the strength to face our temptations and depend on God to strengthen us with the Holy Spirit—and to keep Satan away from us altogether. If you or someone you know is in the grip of sin, then pray for deliverance. Pray that Satan's power will be held back, that his plans will be thwarted, that his grip will be broken.

Verses to study:
> Luke 4:13, 22:31, 32
> Ephesians 6:10-20
> 2 Thessalonians 3:1-2
> 1 Peter 5:8-9.

"For yours is the kingdom, and the power and the glory forever. Amen." Although this phrase is not in some of the earliest manuscripts, it certainly is a fitting ending to the Lord's Prayer. As we conclude our time with God, we return again to praise and glorify him. We remember that the glorious kingdom belongs to God and to no one else. We recognize that *all* power, power beyond our imagination, rests in his hands. We close with our hearts full of praise for God's matchless glory, not wanting it for ourselves, but giving it all to him, who alone is worthy! Amen!

Chapter 15

POUR OUT YOUR HEART

There are times when our heart is so full that it seems as though it is going to break. It may be sorrow, anguish, frustration, guilt, anger—any number of pressures can build up within us until we reach our breaking point. At these times we have a choice to make: We can either try to handle it ourselves, or we can turn to God. And in turning to God, we can either do so superficially, or we can do so deeply. We can choose to merely mention things to God in prayer or we can pour out our hearts.

I am sure that many of us pray about the things that burden us, but fewer of us pour out how we *feel*. David tells us:

> Trust in him at all times, O people;
> > pour out your hearts to him,
> > for God is our refuge (Psalm 62:8).

He says it another way in a later Psalm:

I pour out my complaint before him;
    before him I tell my trouble (Psalm 142:2).

How can we be close to someone to whom we do not pour out our hearts? How can they know us? "But God is all-knowing," we say to ourselves. "He already knows what we think and feel. What's the point of telling him what he already knows?"

To this I say that David and other Bible characters did not look at their relationship with God in such an analytical fashion. They related to him as a child to a father, and what child can be close to a father who does not hear his or her cries? Perhaps God does know how we feel, but unless we tell him our feelings, we will never draw close to him. It is a sad thing that we would be willing to pour out our hearts to a close friend, but withhold those same emotions from our heavenly Father. Such behavior shows how humanistic we are and how impersonal our walk with God is.

Someone else may say, "I'm just not the emotional type. I don't need to cry, and I don't have many feelings to pray about." The fact is, everyone has feelings. It is just that some of us have so long denied them that we do not believe they are there! Also, I would point you to the example of Jesus who both had feelings and expressed them:

> During the days of Jesus' life on earth, he offered up prayers and petitions with loud cries and tears to the one who could save him from death, and he was heard because of his reverent submission (Hebrews 5:7).

Jesus represents the perfect disciple, the person whom we should imitate above all others. We are not following him as we should if we do not allow ourselves to feel and if we do not pour out the contents of our hearts to God.

How can we do this? Let me offer several suggestions:

First, emotion should never be sought as an end in itself, nor should we ever seek to manufacture it. We cannot judge our relationship with God solely by our feelings, but by the standards of Scripture.

Get in the habit of telling God how you feel and expressing your feelings in prayer. The feelings do not have to be sad or distressing; they may be feelings of joy or elation. Express them all.

We usually must be in a place of privacy to be able to express ourselves deeply. If you want to pour out your heart, you will need to be in a place where you feel comfortable doing so.

It often takes a period of time before we can get out of a working or functioning mode and into the "feeling" mode. Give yourself time to unwind, or else you will not be able to commune with God on this level.

It may take an event of crushing impact to bring you to this point. When such times come, do not resent them, rebel against them or harden your heart. Instead, turn to God and pour out your soul in prayer.

Allow yourself to cry. Many of us fight back tears, even as we pray. This is nothing but pride—pride that wants no weakness or vulnerability revealed, even to God. The tears we shed may be tears of despair or tears of sorrow. They may be tears of frustration at prayers that seem thrown back in our faces, apparently unheard. Tears may flow because of a spiritually unresponsive friend or at our own failure to stand against temptation, or at the shame of the utter selfishness of our sin. Thankfully, our tears may be tears of joy—tears such as I shed recently. I was walking down a beautiful wooded path on a spectacular fall day in North Carolina praying through Psalm 68, in which David says of God that he is "a father to the fatherless, a defender of widows" (v5), and it suddenly flashed over me that this verse was written for me and about me—for me, who had lost my dad at twelve and who had lived through most of my teen years alone with my widowed mother. It struck me that

God, even in those years, was looking out for me and for my mother. Caring for us. Protecting us. Preparing me to one day hear the message and respond. When that hit me, I felt a lump in my throat and the warm surging of tears—tears of joy, gratitude and insight—and it felt wonderful! It was one of those times when I felt especially close to God and especially appreciative of something he had done for me, and I will remember always that special moment of closeness to my Father that I enjoyed that day.

∞

We may strive to obey, to be legalistically righteous, but we will never be close to God until we open our hearts and pour out the contents at his feet. Until we do this, we will remain distant. We will feel like a fake, a phony. We will feel artificial. We will remain burdened. And we will be disheartened.

It is a lie to withhold our deepest feelings. We may act as if we are self-sufficient, but we are not. God knows, and in our deepest souls we know. There must be no thought or feeling that we reserve from God. He knows it is there, as do we, and until we talk about it with him, we are distant and dishonest. He already knows it. The sooner we pour it all out, the closer to him we will be.

Chapter 16

PRAY THE PSALMS

One of the most revolutionary events in my life occurred when I discovered the world of praying the Psalms. I do not remember exactly when or how it happened, but I know the profound change it has made in my walk with God.

What do I mean by "praying the Psalms"?

To pray in this manner, select a psalm that most expresses your needs at that particular moment. With your Bible opened up before you, pray your way through that psalm, using it as a guide to expressing your own heart to God. Do not simply read through the psalm as is done in traditional religious services, but use these Spirit-inspired prayers to help you word your own. Put your whole heart and mind into it and see if your expressions to God do not improve dramatically!

This may take some time, and you might feel a bit awkward or artificial at first. I would urge the patience and persistence that is needed in the learning of anything new. Remember, prayer is something we must learn to do (Luke 11:1) which means we must work at it until it becomes natural. Let me offer some suggestions* to get you started:

Psalm 25 is one of my personal favorites, because it is so wide-ranging, allowing us to confess sin, ask for wisdom and express our confidence in God.

Psalm 86 is another great prayer in which we humble ourselves, ask for forgiveness and worship God. I particularly like the requests to "bring joy to your servant" (v4) and to "give me a sign of your goodness" (v17). Also, the plea for God to "give me an undivided heart" (v11) has always been one of my most fervent prayers.

Psalm 103 is a wonderful way to have a prayer of praise. It begins as we speak to our own souls, calling upon ourselves to praise God and to not forget all that God has done. The Spirit then leads us through a series of expressions of gratitude that are absolutely magnificent. In the beginning (v3) we praise God for forgiving us for all our sins. What an incredible thought, and what a great source of joy, when we consider all the sins we have committed! When I come to the next verse which refers to God, who "redeems my life from the pit," I often pray through the entire history of my life, both before and after I became a disciple. I remember when God reached down and found me initially. I remember

---

* *The Leader's Resource Handbook* (Woburn, Mass.: DPI, 1998) has a list of all 150 Psalms broken into prayer categories.

all the people he used to reach me. I also recall all the
countless times since then that he has saved me from
the pits of sin, despair and selfishness. There are many
other great Psalms of praise, and I recommend that you
try them all! I would especially encourage you to pray
through Psalm 145, 148, 65, 66, 96, 23 and 118.

*There are many Psalms that will help you pour out
your heart when you are weak, discouraged or defeated.*
Sometimes I have felt that David must know exactly
what I feel, so well does he express it. Some of the best
Psalms here are 42, 46, 57, 62, 63, 141 and 142.

*The Psalms can teach us how to confess our sin in a
heartfelt way,* so that we arise from prayer knowing that
we have dealt honestly and thoroughly with God about
it. Psalms 32, 38 and 51 are especially helpful here. If
you have sinned grievously, or have lost your heart for
God, praying Psalm 51 can be the way your heart is
made right again.

∾

I cannot tell you all that you need to know here, nor
would I want to. This is a spiritual journey so rich, so
personal and so rewarding that you must take it on your
own. With all my heart I urge you to begin, and to not
give up until you discover what awaits you along the
way.

Chapter 17

PERSONAL

Moses enjoyed a level of intimacy with God that few have ever known. It is said that "The Lord would speak to Moses face to face, as a man speaks with his friend" (Exodus 33:11). Moses would emerge from these divine encounters with his face aglow with the radiance of the glory of God (Exodus 34:29-35). Others walked with God, yet Moses was uniquely close. Why was this? What was it about Moses that caused God to reveal himself to him in an even deeper way than to other great leaders?

There may be other reasons for this, some of which have to do with the level of responsibility and the almost incomprehensible burdens Moses bore, but I see another reason: It was because Moses *wanted* it.

There are two great occasions in Moses' life that illustrate this. The first came after the horrible descent of the Israelites into idolatry. (See Exodus 32 and 33.) After Moses confronts the people and delivers God's judgment for their sin, he returns to speak with God. In his loving concern for the community he asks God to forgive them, and if not, he prays for God to "blot me out of the book you have written" (Exodus 32:32). God graciously honors Moses' request of pardon, and even says he will send an angel with them to give them victory in conquering the promised land (Exodus 33:2). All seems well, but there will be a further consequence. God says, "But I will not go with you" (Exodus 33:2).

How does that sound to you? Would you have accepted this verdict and gone on? "Sounds pretty good to me. At least we are forgiven, and we still get to go to the promised land." Some of us might react that way, but Moses is appalled. He recoils in horror from the thought of losing God's presence. He begs God not to leave them, to go with them. He prays in these immortal words that reveal not only why Moses was a great man, but why he had a great relationship with God:

> Then Moses said to him, "If your Presence does not go with us, do not send us up from here. How will anyone know that you are pleased with me and with your people unless you go with us? What else will distinguish me and your people from all the other people on the face of the earth?" (Exodus 33:15-16).

Do you understand what is happening here? Moses said, in essence, *"It is not enough for us to be forgiven. It is not enough for us to be successful and victorious.*

More important than being blessed by you is knowing *you and being close to you. If you yourself are not going with us, what else makes us any different than anyone else on the face of the earth? Please, please, please go with us!"* This is why Moses was uniquely intimate with God: He valued that intimacy more than anything else! He cared not for success, for glory, for victory or even for pardon if it meant losing the literal, living presence of God.

How about us? I am afraid many of us would have taken God's first offer and would have run. And the fact is, we are doing that very thing right now! We go to church; we sing and clap; we strive to be committed and righteous; we give our money, work hard to share our faith and we even pray; but we are content to do these things, not caring whether we are close to God or not. And that is why, with all the good things we do, there is still something missing. We may be the best version of religious people, but if we lack the true presence of God in our lives, then we will not be deeply, satisfyingly close to our heavenly Father.

To be close to God, we are going to have to start becoming personal with him. We must begin to care everything for the quality of our friendship with God and nothing for the glory of our role. We must be more focused on closeness to God than on the success of our ministry. And do you know what will happen? We will be more committed, active and effective than ever before, but it will be because we are deeply close to God.

Moses' next prayer request tells us even more about his friendship with God. After God promised to personally go with him and the people, Moses had one more prayer to offer: "Now show me your glory" (Exodus 33:18).

Moses, despite all he knew of God, hungered for more. He longed for a deeper experience and knowledge of God himself. A true man or woman of God is one who loves and adores God *for God himself.* And that is why Moses was so close to God—because more than all else in his life, that is what he desired.

Paul, in 2 Corinthians 3, says that in Jesus we have a greater revelation, covenant and opportunity than Moses had. He says that, unlike Moses, our glory does not fade and the least of us in God's kingdom today has the wonderful opportunity of close fellowship with God.

I remember reading the story of Moses as a young disciple and having to deal with feelings of envy as I longed for such a profound closeness to God myself. I now realize that I, too, can be the friend of God—such an incredible blessing is now not only the possession of the great lawgiver Moses, but of any disciple of Jesus.

I want to urge you to become personal with God, to value above all else your relationship with him, to pour your whole heart into it and to never, ever let it fade away!

Chapter 18

POINTED

Once Jesus was beseeched from the roadside by two blind men who cried out, "Have mercy on us!" As the crowd attempted to silence them, they only shouted louder, "Have mercy on us!" His attention arrested, Jesus asked them a simple but profound question, "What is it you want me to do for you?" (Matthew 20:29-34).

We cannot be close to God in prayer if we deal only in generalities. *"Bless me, Lord; bless my family; and bless our church..."* we may pray. To which the Lord is likely saying, "Just *how* would you like me to bless you and all these people?" You see, God indeed wants to answer our prayers, but unless we become specific in our requests, how will we know if our prayers are actually getting through and what God is really doing?

Abraham gives us a powerful example of just how specific our prayers can be. In Genesis 18 is recorded one of·the most remarkable prayers in the Bible. Angelic messengers have revealed to Abraham that Sodom, the home of his nephew Lot, is such a wicked city that the Lord is soon going to destroy it. We will see from what is about to transpire that it is not without reason that this man is called the friend of God (2 Chronicles 20:7). Abraham, in a prayer that shows an amazing combination of boldness, humility and familiarity with God, approaches the Lord to ask him to reconsider:

> Then Abraham approached him and said: "Will you sweep away the righteous with the wicked? What if there are fifty righteous people in the city? Will you really sweep it away and not spare the place for the sake of the fifty righteous people in it? Far be it from you to do such a thing—to kill the righteous with the wicked, treating the righteous and the wicked alike. Far be it from you! Will not the Judge of all the earth do right?" (Genesis 18:23-25).

The Lord agrees to his request, but Abraham is not done yet. He continues his requests, each time lowering the number of righteous people there would have to be before God would act. First, he gets God to go down to forty-five, then forty. His boldness increasing, he makes a subtraction of ten...then, upon obtaining another "Yes," he goes for ten less! He takes a deep breath, prays again, and upon receiving another positive answer, finally decides to leave well enough alone at ten righteous souls in Sodom! But Sodom's name is not associated with evil for nothing—there were not even ten decent people in the whole city when it was destroyed.

A relationship as familiar as Abraham had with God is unfortunately beyond the comprehension (and experience) of many of us. But it should not be! Jesus said that the Father in heaven knows when the sparrow falls, and that we are much more valuable than a sparrow (Matthew 10:29-31). Paul said in Philippians 4:6,

> Do not be anxious about anything, but in everything, by prayer and petition, with thanksgiving, present your requests to God.

If the word "anything" means the same to you as it does to me, then it is time to become pointed in our prayers!

If our lack of specific praying reveals a distance in our relationship with God, it also can be the way we turn the problem around. We can get closer to God by becoming more pointed in our prayer lives. Learn to be more specific in your gratitude. Express specifically those people, situations, and blessings for which you are thankful. Do the same in your confession of sin. Get to the point. Express in clear biblical terminology the sin of which you are guilty. In your requests for God to bless the lives of you and your friends, be exact in what you ask for. The same holds true in your desire to be fruitful in evangelism. For example, I am asking God to grant me an effective and fruitful ministry in the sports I am the most involved in: weight training, running and golf. A young man I met at the gym became a disciple earlier, and now I am asking God to use me in even greater ways as I reach out to the people I meet in these activities. (I have also asked to be phenomenally great in all three sports, as well, but like Abraham at the number ten, I think I have pushed the Lord as far as I can!)

As we grow closer to God, we become more specific in prayer, and as we become more specific in prayer, we grow closer to God. Like Abraham, the great friend of God, let us humbly, boldly and specifically lay out our requests before our loving Father in heaven.

Chapter 19

PERSISTENCE

God values persistence in our prayers. Jesus even told a parable with the lesson that we "should always pray and not give up" (Luke 18:1).

Disciples who are not close to God are simply not being persistent. Somewhere along the line we have given up, and that "somewhere" is usually in our prayer lives. Perhaps we feel we have prayed and prayed and still we are unheard. Perhaps we have become rote in our manner of prayer and need to change. Perhaps we wonder if God is tired of hearing the some old requests day in and day out.

We must never give up praying! The Bible is full of examples to inspire us to keep on praying, no matter how tempted we may be to quit. Remember that Elisha had to pray seven times before the promised rainfall came down (1 Kings 18:42-45). Recall that Jesus returned three times to pour out his heart to God in the garden of Gethsemane before he was entirely surrendered to God's will (Matthew 26:36ff). Remember that Paul had to pray three times before being given a definitive answer— and it was not the one he wanted!—concerning his thorn in the flesh (2 Corinthians 12:7-9). Remember that the answer to Daniel's prayer was delayed twenty-one days because of Satanic opposition (Daniel 10:1-14). Do not forget that the church gathered and prayed all night for Peter's deliverance from imprisonment and death (Acts 12:1-17). And remember that Jesus powerfully emphasized persistence in his teaching on prayer (Luke 11: 5-13, 18:1-8).

Some prayers will be prayed over and over because they are prayers of relationship (i.e. thanksgiving, praise) and not requests. Other prayers are those we pray continually for loved ones, as we unabatedly bring their names and needs before the throne of God. Others are prayers for the lost, perhaps for friends and family who are as yet unresponsive to the Gospel, and we never stop praying that somehow, some way, God will open their hearts. Still others are prayers for God to right a wrong, to strengthen us against temptation or to bring some great thing to pass. These are the persistent prayers of a lifetime. These are the prayers we must pray, pray some more and pray for years and pray even with our last breath on earth!

Chapter 20

POSTURES

Prayer is an activity that involves not only our minds and hearts, but our bodies as well. As we look at prayer and praying saints in the Bible, we find that they fully employed their bodies in prayer—often in very dramatic fashion. If we are to be men and women who communicate deeply with God, then we must imitate their example.

What are some of the postures of prayer that we see in the Scriptures?

Kneeling. Perhaps no posture is more associated with prayer than this. Solomon knelt and prayed (1 Kings 8:54), as did the prophet Elijah, with his face between his knees (1 Kings 18:42). Daniel knelt in prayer three times a day before an open window (Daniel 6:10). The Gospels are replete with examples of people kneeling before Jesus to ask for healings or other blessings. Peter knelt in prayer as he pled for the life of Tabitha (Acts 9:40), and Paul fell on his knees in worship as he considered the greatness of God's love in Christ (Ephesians 3:14).

Standing. Jesus gave instructions that when we "stand praying" we should forgive (Mark 11:25) and told a parable in which the contrite tax collector stood in prayer but would not look up to heaven (Luke 18:13).

Prostrate. Moses lay prostrate before God for forty days and nights (Deuteronomy 9:18, 25). Daniel fell prostrate before the angel Gabriel (Daniel 8:17), and David and the people fell prostrate before the Lord in praise (1 Chronicles 29:20). Jesus fell on his face in prayer as he surrendered his will to God in the garden of Gethsemane (Matthew 26:36ff).

Lifting and spreading out hands. We have many examples of this in the Psalms (28:2, 63:4, 88:9, 119:48, 143:6) and from other Biblical characters like Ezra (Ezra 9:5), Moses (Exodus 9:29) and Solomon (1 Kings 8:22). The early church was told to lift "holy hands" in prayer (1 Timothy 2:8).

Gazing upward. We have already seen an example of looking down, away from heaven (Luke 18:13). We have instances of Jesus looking up to heaven in prayer (Matthew 14:19, Mark 6: 41, 7:34).

Dramatic postures and actions. In times of extreme distress or grief, or as a sign of deep self-abasement, people would tear their clothing and put on sackcloth, which they would sometimes wear for many days. This was often accompanied by placing dust on their heads. (Genesis 37:34, Numbers 14:6, Joshua 7:6, 2 Samuel 1:11,

Nehemiah 9:1, Esther 4:1ff, Daniel 9:3, Acts 14:14). King Hezekiah, when he received the threatening letter from the Assyrian king Sennacherib, not only put on sackcloth but took the letter and spread it out before the Lord as he prayed for deliverance (see Isaiah 36, 37).

Praying aloud. Prayers were offered silently (1 Samuel 1:13) or aloud, sometimes with a very loud voice (Esther 4:1, Hebrews 5:7, James 4:7-9).

What do all of these examples teach us? It is clear that prayer is offered up in many ways, according to whatever best expresses the need of the hour. As our prayers come from our hearts and are offered in different circumstances in our lives, they will take many forms. If our prayers are not offered from a variety of postures, then we are not praying as we ought.

When is the last time you fell prostrate before God? When is the last time you prayed in a loud voice or fell on your knees? We cannot separate our bodies from our hearts. Certainly someone could put on a hypocritical performance of prayer, but most of us desperately need to be more demonstrative. Our lack of body language in speaking with God betrays our lukewarm, anemic prayer life.

I remember a time in my life when my friends Kip McKean and Al Baird challenged me to face my need to become a stronger leader—a leader of impact who preached God's word fearlessly and powerfully. I was so moved that I returned to my home, went down to the basement, laid face down on the concrete floor and cried tears of repentance, as I promised God that I would become the man he wanted me to be. I came up out of the basement, called my family together, informed them of my repentance and went on to make the needed changes. I look back on that prayer as one of the most crucial in my life, a prayer that set a new course for my future.

Find your own ways to pray effectively. Many disciples have found that taking a prayer walk outdoors is a great way to pray. I have developed the ability to pray with great concentration and intimacy as I run. In training for a recent marathon, I found this to be a wonderful way to fellowship with God, especially as I went on long outdoor runs early in the morning. For some of us who have a hard time staying awake when we pray, learning to converse with God while walking or running may be just the answer for which we have been searching.

I would urge you to be more heartfelt, more humble, more creative and more dramatic in your prayers. Get on your knees. Pray out loud. Raise your voice. Shed some tears. Spread out your hands or raise them up to God. Look up into the heavens in praise; look down to the earth in humility. Get out of your dull routine: Put your whole mind, soul, heart and body into your prayers, and see what happens!

Chapter 21

PRAISE

Praise and thanksgiving are prayer at its highest. Praise is the song sung daily by nature and by the countless inhabitants of heaven. Never are we more right with God than when we overflow with gratitude and thanksgiving, and never are we more what we are created to be than when we praise, magnify and glorify God.

Thanksgiving is praise made practical. In thanksgiving we express our appreciation for what God has done. Paul's letters are full of thanksgiving, and of admonitions for us to be grateful. Consider these, from one of the shortest of Paul's letters, the letter to the Colossians (emphases mine):

We always thank God, the Father of our Lord Jesus Christ, when we pray for you (Colossians 1:3).

So then, just as you received Christ Jesus as Lord, continue to live in him, rooted and built up in him, strengthened in the faith as you were taught, and *overflowing with thankfulness* (Colossians 2:6-7).

Let the peace of Christ rule in your hearts, since as members of one body you were called to peace. *And be thankful* (Colossians 3:15).

Devote yourselves to prayer, *being watchful and thankful* (Colossians 4:2).

We should overflow with gratitude. It should not be an occasional expression, but should permeate our prayer lives. And it is something we can work on, a practice and attitude that we can cultivate.

What should we be grateful for? We should thank God for answered prayers, for the blessings of friends and family, for our health, for material blessings, for the joys of being in God's kingdom, for those who have spiritually helped us...for all of this and much more, we should be thankful.

We will find that as we articulate our thanksgiving, our eyes are opened to all that God has done and given. Our appreciation grows, our anxiety decreases, and our joy abounds. As we learn to express thanks regardless of how we feel at the moment, we find our mood improving. I am convinced that for some un-happy, sourpuss disciples, their only hope of change is to become grateful. I have never known a person habitually expressive of gratitude to be afflicted with continual discouragement and depression.

Where better to be thankful to God than in speaking to him in prayer? But this will take conscious effort. Our faithless anxiety and our selfish tendency to continually focus on our own needs will not easily go away. I would suggest some prayer times in which you devote at least half, or perhaps all, of the session to thanksgiving. If you take prayer walks, decide occasionally to begin your prayer with thanksgiving and to make no requests until you are more than halfway through your walk. As I have prayed during training runs, I have begun to notice that my prayers of thanksgiving and praise have taken up more and more of the early miles of my run. I welcome this as a sign of growth in my attitude of gratitude.

Work on this however you wish, and see if it does not leave you in an entirely different frame of mind when you are done praying. If you are like many people, your faith will be so much greater after expressing thanks that by the time you begin to lay your requests before God, your confidence will be at an all-time high! I would also suggest keeping a "gratitude list" of answered prayers and other blessings for which you regularly thank God.

If thanksgiving is the expression of appreciation for what God has *done,* praise is the grateful, exalted recognition of who God *is.*

Paul seems to spontaneously break forth in praise as he writes his letters:

Oh, the depth of the riches of the wisdom
     and knowledge of God!
   How unsearchable his judgments,
   and his paths beyond tracing out!
"Who has known the mind of the Lord?
   Or who has been his counselor?"
"Who has ever given to God,
   that God should repay him?"
For from him and through him and to him are all things.
   To him be the glory forever! Amen
(Romans 11:33-36).

Whenever you see the phrase "thanks be to God" in one of Paul's letters, prepare for an outpouring of praise! I would encourage more of this exuberant, happy spirit, especially in our prayer lives.

Jesus was the same way. When the seventy-two returned from their mission, Jesus was so moved that he could not hold back his praise:

At that time Jesus, full of joy through the Holy Spirit, said, "I praise you, Father, Lord of heaven and earth, because you have hidden these things from the wise and learned, and revealed them to little children. Yes, Father, for this was your good pleasure" (Luke 10:21).

❧

God's world sings out his praise every day and every night. All that he has made, in its vastness, intricacy and beauty shouts out the greatness and glory of God. If all of nature from time immemorial has joined in a symphony of glorious praise, then how much more should we! There is no greater thing we can ever do or say, than to praise God. And there is no time when we are nearer to him than when we pour forth the high praises of him, our glorious Father in Heaven. As the prophet said,

> "You will go out in joy
>   and be led forth in peace;
> the mountains and hills
>   will burst into song before you,
> and all the trees of the field
>   will clap their hands.
> Instead of the thornbush will grow the pine tree,
>   and instead of briers the myrtle will grow.
> This will be for the LORD's renown,
>   for an everlasting sign,
> which will not be destroyed" (Isaiah 55:12-13).

Chapter 22

PSALMS YOU SING

Music has always been a part of the worship of God and of drawing near to God. In our corporate worship, we experience the incredible impact music has upon us as we sing, as we listen to others sing and as we hear the accompanying instruments. Nothing is quite as effective as music in improving our moods or softening our hearts.

David sang to God as he kept his lonely vigil in the hills of Bethlehem. The psalms he created have changed the world and have drawn millions closer to God. Many of those beautiful songs were composed and sung as he gave forth his private worship. What better way for him to spend his time than in writing, playing and singing songs to God? Perhaps it was this that caused God to send Samuel to anoint David as king because "the LORD looks at the heart" (1 Samuel 16:7). Let's look at some great psalms that include verses about singing to God:

My heart is steadfast, O God,
  my heart is steadfast;
I will sing and make music (Psalm 57:7).

Then my head will be exalted
  above the enemies who surround me;
at his tabernacle will I sacrifice with shouts of joy;
  I will sing and make music to the Lord (Psalm 27:6).

It is good to praise the Lord
  and make music to your name, O Most High
(Psalm 92:1).

Let us come before him with thanksgiving
  and extol him with music and song (Psalm 95:2).

Shout for joy to the Lord, all the earth,
  burst into jubilant song with music;
make music to the Lord with the harp,
  with the harp and the sound of singing (Psalm 98:4-5).

My heart is steadfast, O God;
  I will sing and make music with all my soul (Psalm 108:1).

The use of music in our personal devotions is of utmost importance and is possessed of immense power. Music opens up our hearts and frees us from a mere intellectual approach. In song we engage our minds, emotions and hearts as we worship. Music is both humbling and exalting—humbling in that we assume a true attitude of worship when we sing (especially if we are vocally challenged!), and exalting in that we free our hearts to worship unfettered by stuffy intellectualism.

Procure a songbook and start singing during your quiet times! Do not be concerned about how you sound to yourself; only be concerned about pleasing the heart of God.

I would encourage you to play inspiring or worshipful recorded music as you study and meditate. I have found this to be of limitless value in helping me to relax, to get into the proper frame of mind (and stay there!) and to help in eliminating distractions. Our family has also found that playing this type of music helps to set a better atmosphere in our home and in our car as we travel. There are many outstanding classical and contemporary works that are available, and I would urge you to invest the time and money to build a collection.

If your relationship with God seems dry and lifeless, music may be the missing element, as it was at one time for me. Then one day as I was reading, this verse jumped out at me:

The LORD is my strength and my song;
    he has become my salvation (Psalm 118:14).

As I read with a new insight, I realized that I had allowed God in my life only as my strength, not as my strength *and* my song. I decided to change and learn to have a singing heart. I began to work on it and pray about it, asking God to help me transform my heart and attitude. I certainly have not yet arrived, but that prayer is being answered! God is much more my song than he ever has been before. I urge you: Let God not only be your strength, but your song as well. Open your heart and your mouth and sing! Then you can join with David as he sings,

> "You turned my wailing into dancing;
>   you removed my sackcloth and clothed me with joy,
> that my heart may sing to you and not be silent.
>   O Lord my God, I will give you thanks forever"
> (Psalm 30:11-12).

Epilogue

I trust that the reading of this book has encouraged, enlightened and inspired you. I want to leave you with one word of caution.

Do not seek to build a relationship with God based on your feelings. It would be a grave mistake for you to read this book and then go about seeking to experience a spiritual high in every time of prayer or every session of Bible study. We should seek for closeness to God and not for some special sense of his presence. I believe that we need times of "feeling" close to God, and we should have many. If we never have them, something is amiss. I also believe that many disciples are harmed by the misbelief that unless they have a special, mystical feeling of closeness, that they have not adequately prayed or they have not learned anything.

In my own prayers and studies, I do not always walk away with a great feeling of having learned something new or having been brought to the very throne of God. I do strive to leave those times knowing that I have sincerely and genuinely given my heart and mind to God. On occasion, I leave my quiet times with a sense of frustration or disappointment that they did not go better. Upon later reflection, I have wondered if some of those were not times that God thought things actually went very well, indeed.

Feelings are tricky things. If we never have them in our relationship with God, then I would question whether or not we are genuinely close to him. But if we depend on them as the barometer of how we are doing spiritually, we are headed for trouble. Rather than seeking feelings, seek God's kingdom and his righteousness. Rather than seeking a thrilling moment, seek to know the God of heaven. Rather than looking for a warm glow, seek to have a heart afire with conviction. And then, whatever your feelings may be, you can know that you have been still before God, that he is in your heart and that you are walking with him.

> "Be still, and know that I am God;
>   I will be exalted among the nations,
>   I will be exalted in the earth" (Psalm 46:10).

DISCIPLESHIP
PUBLICATIONS
INTERNATIONAL

Who Are We?

Discipleship Publications International (DPI) began publishing in 1993. We are a non-profit Christian publisher committed to publishing and distributing materials that honor God, lift up Jesus Christ and show how his message practically applies to all areas of life. We have a deep conviction that no one changes life like Jesus and that the implementation of his teaching will revolutionize any life, any marriage, any family and any singles household.

Since our beginning we have published more than 75 titles; plus we have produced a number of important, spiritual audio products. More than one million volumes have been printed, and our works have been translated into more than a dozen languages—international is not just a part of our name! Our books are shipped monthly to every inhabited continent.

To see a more detailed description of our works, find us on the World Wide Web at **www.dpibooks.com**. You can order books listed on the following pages by calling 1-888-DPI-BOOK 24 hours per day. From outside the US, call 781-937-3883, ext. 231 during Boston-area business hours.

We appreciate the hundreds of comments we have received from readers. We would love to hear from you. Here are other ways to get in touch:

Mail: DPI, One Merrill St., Woburn, MA 01801
E-mail: dpibooks@icoc.org

The Promises of God

Edited by Thomas and Sheila Jones

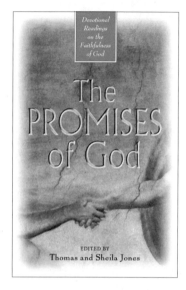

The Bible is filled with what Peter calls "great and precious promises" from God. In this book, leaders from around the world examine some of these promises and show how trusting in them gives strength, confidence and calm to our hearts and minds. God has given us his promises to encourage us and give us a reason to never ever give up. This book will give loads of encouragement to those who read it. As you will read in the opening chapter:

Nothing is more at the heart of this book than this idea: God fulfills his promises—every last one of them. The last man you voted for may not have done a very good job doing what he promised, but God is not like that man or like any man. He is trustworthy, reliable and absolutely faithful to every promise he makes. And since he is God, he has the power to do what he has promised to do. A promise from God is as good as a fact. You can rely on it. You can build on it. You can act on it. You can stand on it.

Letters to New Disciples

BY THOMAS A. JONES

In this book, DPI's editor-in-chief addresses twenty-four vital issues faced by new Christians and helps them see God's plan for winning the battles. The most difficult time for new Christians is in their first few months as a disciple. This book is designed to help them through those early challenges.

The Spirit
The Work of the Holy Spirit in the Lives of Disciples

BY DOUGLAS JACOBY

The Spirit is really two books in one. In Part One Douglas shows in practical ways how to walk in the Spirit and live in the Spirit's power. In Part Two the reader will find a more technical discussion of many issues connected with the Charismatic and Neopentecostal movements of the twentieth century as well as Biblical answers to a host of other questions. For all of those who want a sound understanding of the living water that Jesus promised (John 7:38), this book will meet many needs.

The Killer Within
An African Look at Disease, Sin and Keeping Yourself Saved

BY MIKE TALIAFERRO

What do the Ebola virus, cholera, meningitis and the Guinea worm have to do with sin? In this poignant book you will find out. Mike Taliaferro has done it again! In his unique style he uses the physical world to paint a vivid picture of the deeper, more crucial issue of sin's effect on the soul. Powerful images of disease and sickness drive home the conviction that sin must never be taken lightly.

The Leader's Resource Handbook,
Volume One

A unique collection of materials from a variety of leaders in one handy volume. This material will train, equip, inspire and motivate. Great for those leading small groups as well as for full-time leaders leading larger ministries. Spiral-bound.

Walking with God

BY RUSS EWELL

Russ Ewell, one of the most dynamic speakers in the kingdom of God, shows that a relationship with God is the most exciting thing a human being can do with his life. Topics include (1) Wrestling with God, (2) Walking with God and (3) One Holy Passion. A DPI best-seller. 3-cassette series.

After God's Own Heart

Lessons from the Life of David

BY SAM LAING

Scripture says he was "a man after God's own heart." What a tribute! From his days as a shepherd boy to his reign as Israel's king, David poured out his heart to God, demonstrated an amazing heart toward his best friend and to his worst enemy, struggled with sin that crept into his own heart, and wrote songs and psalms that still move our hearts three thousand years later. In this four-cassette series Sam Laing speaks with warmth, humor and deep conviction, showing today's disciples what they can learn from David's intensely personal walk with God. 4-cassette series.

Generation Next

There is a spiritual battle raging for the minds and souls of preteens and teens. Parents must not be deceived; they must get in the fight for their children's faith. In the midst of all the world's influences, the greatest influence in a child's life is his or her parents and their spirituality.

These messages contain practical solutions and answers that make winning the battle possible. The call is for parents to run to the fight armed with the weapons of God. 4-cassette series.

Born Free

BY RYAN HOWARD

Three life-changing messages that will radically transform how you view who you are in Christ, how you can have confidence in your walk with God, and how to enjoy your life as a child of God. 3-cassette series.